A Spiritual Formation
Workbook

Other RENOVARÉ Resources for Spiritual Renewal:

Devotional Classics
Embracing the Love of God
Songs for Renewal
Streams of Living Water
A Spiritual Formation Journal
Wilderness Time

A Spiritual Formation Workbook

SMALL-GROUP RESOURCES FOR

NURTURING CHRISTIAN GROWTH

A REVISED EDITION

James Bryan Smith
with Lynda L. Graybeal

FOREWORD BY
Richard J. Foster

A RENOVARÉ RESOURCE FOR SPIRITUAL RENEWAL

HarperSanFrancisco
A Division of HarperCollinsPublishers

For information about RENOVARÉ write to RENOVARÉ, 8 Inverness Drive East, Suite 102, Englewood, CO 80112-5624 USA.

HarperCollins books may be purchased for educational, business, or sales promotional use. For information please write: Special Markets Department, HarperCollins Publishers, Inc., 10 East 53rd Street, New York, NY 10022.

HarperCollins Web Site: http://www.harpercollins.com

HarperCollins®, ☰®, and HarperSanFrancisco™ are trademarks of HarperCollins Publishers Inc.

FIRST HARPERSANFRANCISCO EDITION PUBLISHED 1993

Library of Congress Cataloging-in-Publication Data
Smith, James Bryan.
    A spiritual formation workbook: small-group resources for nurturing Christian growth / James Bryan Smith; foreword by Richard J. Foster. — Rev. ed.
      p. cm.
   ISBN 0–06–251626–4
    1. Spiritual formation. 2. Church group work. I. Title.
BV4511.S65 1999
253'.7—dc20   92–36860
     06 05 04 ❖/RRD(H) 20

To my parents,
Calvin and Wanda Smith

Special thanks to Richard J. Foster for the concept of the Six Traditions, his friendship, and his insight into the nature of spiritual growth; Lynda Graybeal for her oversight and updating of this whole project; Virginia Stem Owens for her expertise in line editing; Greg May for his wonderful initial graphic design and icons; Kandace Hawkinson and the people of HarperSanFrancisco for their belief in RENOVARÉ; my wife, Meghan, for her support and encouragement; and all of the Spiritual Formation Groups whose contributions were an essential part of this effort.

James Bryan Smith

Contents

Foreword   9

Introduction   11

Starting a Group   15

EIGHT BEGINNING SESSIONS   23
Becoming a Spiritual Formation Group

Session 1   **Discovering a Balanced Vision of Christian Faith and Practice**   25
The Life of Jesus Christ

Session 2   **Practicing the Prayer-Filled Life**   32
The Contemplative Tradition

Session 3   **Practicing the Virtuous Life**   37
The Holiness Tradition

Session 4   **Practicing the Spirit-Empowered Life**   44
The Charismatic Tradition

Session 5   **Practicing the Compassionate Life**   51
The Social Justice Tradition

Session 6   **Practicing the Word-Centered Life**   59
The Evangelical Tradition

Session 7   **Practicing the Sacramental Life**   *67*
                     The Incarnational Tradition

Session 8   **Discovering a Practical Strategy for Spiritual Growth**   *74*
                     The Spiritual Formation Group

                     Periodic Evaluation   *81*

                     Ideas and Exercises   *86*

                     Order of Meeting   *99*

                     Worksheet   *103*

                     Bibliography   *105*

                     RENOVARÉ   *109*

Foreword

For some time I participated in two Spiritual Formation Groups simultaneously and was immeasurably enriched by both experiences. The first group was composed of only myself and one other person, the author of this book. The second included myself and three other individuals.

In the fall of 1988, Jim Smith and I started meeting just to see how a nurturing fellowship of mutual accountability might work. I cannot tell you how encouraging and fun-filled those first meetings were: we laughed at our foibles and rejoiced in our successes; we prayed; we made confession; we brought the grace of forgiveness; we made mutual covenants; we challenged and encouraged each other. They were high, holy, hilarious times.

In time, Jim and I were led to study many small-group movements, such as the Benedictines in the sixth century, the Franciscans in the thirteenth century, the Methodists in the eighteenth century, and Alcoholics Anonymous in the twentieth century. We also began developing a balanced vision of Christian faith and practice and a practical strategy for spiritual growth.

The second group came a bit later, and now a third has developed, but each has been equally encouraging. Why do I continue to be in Spiritual Formation Groups? Briefly, let me explain why they mean so much to me.

First, I like the sense of community. None of us is supposed to live the Christian life alone. We gain strength and help from others.

Second, I like the nurturing character. The rule for our weekly gatherings is a good one: give encouragement as often as possible; advice, once in a great while; reproof, only when absolutely necessary; and judgment, *never*.

Third, I like the intentionality. Our purpose is to become better disciples of Jesus Christ. Everything is oriented around this single goal.

Fourth, I like the loving accountability. I need others to ask hard questions about my prayer experiences, temptations and struggles, and plans for spiritual growth.

Fifth, I like the balanced vision. To be baptized into the great streams of Christian faith and practice helps free me from my many provincialisms.

Sixth, I like the practical strategy. I want and need realistic handles that actually move me forward into Christlikeness.

Seventh, I like the freedom and the fun. These groups encourage discipline without rigidity, accountability without manipulation.

I enthusiastically recommend this workbook to you. It is the fruit of extensive study and research into group dynamics and the nature of spiritual development. It also has the ambience of those early meetings Jim and I had together. And though I have moved some distance from Jim geographically and we are no longer able to meet together, I still remember well those early days of high, holy hilarity!

Richard J. Foster

Introduction

WHAT IS RENOVARÉ?

RENOVARÉ (Latin meaning "to renew") is committed to the renewal of the Church of Jesus Christ in all her multifaceted expressions. An "infrachurch" effort, it focuses on helping bring renewal to local churches.

The mission of RENOVARÉ is to provide individual churches and their members with a balanced, practical, effective small-group strategy for spiritual growth. These "Spiritual Formation Groups" give depth to our desire for God and increase the level of our discipleship. While it is impossible to measure spiritual growth, those who have been part of a Spiritual Formation Group for a six-month trial period describe a marked change in their lives. One woman notes, "Since I started a group with one other woman in my church, my life of discipleship has grown one hundred percent."

A pastor of a large inner-city church has been developing Spiritual Formation Groups in his church since 1989 because he feels that "they are an indispensable tool of discipleship for the end of the twentieth century." His goal is to have every member of his church in a Spiritual Formation Group by the year 2000.

WHY DOES THE RENOVARÉ PLAN AID SPIRITUAL GROWTH?

The secret of the program is the combination of three very important ingredients. The first is *balance*. To be spiritually healthy, we need balance in our spiritual lives, just as physical health needs balance in diet and exercise. Founded upon the six major areas of discipline found in the life of Jesus Christ and the corresponding Six Traditions seen in the history of the Church, RENOVARÉ emphasizes balance.

The second ingredient is *knowledge*. Many of us do not become a disciple of Jesus for one reason: we lack information about how to do the spiritual disciplines. We dream about being true followers, imagine ourselves being committed disciples, but what do we actually *do?* What steps do we take? What activities do we engage in that will help us grow closer to God? We are like travelers looking across a great chasm, longing for the other side, discontent with where we are, yet unable to cross the bridge because we do not know how to start. The RENOVARÉ program provides that knowledge: what to do and how to do it.

The third ingredient is *mutual encouragement and accountability*. Once we find a balanced plan and gain knowledge of how to use it, the only thing left for us is to *do* it. Unfortunately, for most of us this is the hardest part. Ingrained habits hamper us from changing the way we are. The secret to breaking these ingrained habits is the strength found in joining forces with others who have a similar mission. They provide the encouragement we need to start across the chasm and the accountability we need to keep us on the bridge. RENOVARÉ's strategy utilizes the God-given strength we gain from each other.

HOW DOES A SPIRITUAL FORMATION GROUP WORK?

From two to seven people gather regularly to study, to share their past experiences, and to make plans for the week ahead. This is done easily by following a suggested Order of Meeting.

During each gathering (which should last between sixty and ninety minutes) one person is designated as that week's leader. He or she guides the group through a series of opening words, a question-and-answer session, and a closing time of prayer. Within this flexible format, members are reminded of their task, enabled to hear from one another, and empowered to share, plan, and dream with each other. It is within this framework that the balance, the knowledge, and the encouragement and accountability are nurtured.

HOW DO I USE THIS WORKBOOK?

The plan itself is very simple. However, you must take a few steps to get a Spiritual Formation Group started.

- *Find a partner or partners.*
  The next section of this workbook, "Starting a Group," offers helpful insights about how to bring a group together. Please note that at this stage, you are looking for one to six other people who are willing to gather for nine weeks to "test-drive" this strategy. At this point, that is all you are asking them to do.

- *Educate yourself and the group members.*
  At least one or maybe all Spiritual Formation Group members lack the first two ingredients necessary for spiritual growth: balance and knowledge. This workbook contains eight sessions that will provide these two ingredients.

  Session 1 provides your group with the "big picture"—that is, our model, Jesus Christ, and our illustration, the Six Traditions of the Church. Sessions 2 through 7 provide a basic understanding of six areas of discipline that make up our balanced diet, along with an explanation of how they function in our lives. Session 8 brings it all together, providing you with the tools you will need to be an ongoing group in the future—if your group chooses to continue. We encourage you to meet one more time (Session 9), using the Order of Meeting, to give the regular group meeting a try.

- *Decide whether or not to continue meeting.*
  After the group has gone through the nine-week trial period, it will have (1) a functional knowledge of the Six Traditions, (2) a knowledge of how those Traditions are woven into our daily lives, (3) practical experience in each area, and (4) a sense of how working as a group enhances our ability to accomplish our goals.

  At this point—either at the end of the trial regular meeting or at a separate tenth meeting—the Spiritual Formation Group will need to decide its future by working through the chapter titled "Periodic Evaluation," answering a series of questions designed to help the group plan for its future. We have found it best for those who are willing to continue meeting to make a six-month commitment to this program. At the end of the six months, the group can reevaluate themselves once again, using the same process.

  Should any member or members of the group decide to stop here, or should the entire group decide to disband, the evaluation and planning process provides a graceful way to leave or break up. No group or individual should feel pressure to continue in a plan that does not meet their needs. We realize that this program will not fit everyone. Even groups that meet over many years need to remember the importance of periodic evaluation.

WHAT SHOULD I DO NEXT?

If you decide that you would like to form a Spiritual Formation Group, read through several of the sessions on your own. Most certainly, these can be used by individuals as a personal study, but we offer this counsel: just as it "takes two to tango," so also it "takes (at least) two to covenant." In other words, the sessions work best when done in the context of a group of two or more so that the members can share and plan and lovingly hold one another accountable. We do encourage the organizer to study the sessions before meeting with a group, however.

A WORD OF ENCOURAGEMENT

If you have decided to try this strategy, please keep in mind that we at RENOVARÉ have no desire to control your actions or to demand that you use this program exactly as it was designed. We are committed to the Church, and this plan is our gift to the Church.

Furthermore, we are not concerned that you use the RENOVARÉ name for your group or groups within your church; some simply use the name "Spiritual Formation Group." For you to grow closer to God and to your Christian sisters and brothers is our heart's desire. We cheerfully offer you and your church this theologically sound and experientially effective small-group strategy—a strategy that grew out of doing research over the years, listening to God, and responding to the needs of people.

Now turn to the next section, titled "Starting a Group," to find suggestions for forming a Spiritual Formation Group. May God bless you richly in this endeavor.

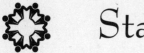 # Starting a Group

Since you are reading this workbook, we know that you have caught the vision of a mobilized Church going out into the world and making "disciples of all nations," permanently changing that world for the better (Matt. 28:19b). While the Church has spread organically around the world, on an individual level it seems to be failing to "make disciples." About this, philosopher and writer Dallas Willard says, "Our existing churches and denominations do not have active, well-designed, intently pursued plans to accomplish [fulfilling the Great Commission] in their members. . . . [Y]ou will not find any widely influential element of our church leadership that has a plan—not a vague wish or dream, but a *plan* for implementing *all* phases of the Great Commission" (*The Spirit of the Disciplines*, p. 167).

We at RENOVARÉ believe that the strategy presented here—Spiritual Formation Groups where Christians meet to learn the Six Traditions of the Church, to do the related disciplines, to hold each other accountable, and to encourage one another—makes disciples. And incorporating the RENOVARÉ materials into an existing group or starting a Spiritual Formation Group is much easier than you might think.

The following guidelines will help you put a group together.

WORKING WITH AN EXISTING GROUP

If you are already meeting in a small group not formally affiliated with a church (or affiliated with a church but independently guided) and would like to see this material used, begin by praying about the idea. Trust God to guide you for the right time to approach the leader or (if you are the leader) the members and ask if they would like to try out a nine-session Spiritual Formation Group. If the leader or group answers no, relax and thank God that you are in a small group where you can have fellowship and companionship in your Christian walk. If the answer is yes, thank God for the opening and ask the leader if you can help get the materials together; if you are the leader, start making plans for the first session. (Alternatively, you could simply integrate individual aspects of this program into your existing structure and format.)

STARTING A NEW GROUP

Starting a new group is a little more complicated, but we hope the following guidelines will help you. Again, begin by asking the Lord for guidance. If the answer is no, continue to pray for a door to open that will bring other opportunities for spiritual growth into your life. If the answer is yes, thank God for his faithfulness in providing spiritual nurture for you and start working through the following steps.

Involve Your Church Staff

If you want to start a group in your own church, the expertise and encouragement of the pastor or priest and other leaders will be invaluable. They are responsible for the spiritual health of "the flock" and are therefore very concerned that members take part in helpful programs. We suggest that you ask them to look over this workbook and any other RENOVARÉ materials you may have.

Doing this is not merely a common courtesy; it is essential if the plan is to have a positive effect on your church. The pastoral staff is ultimately responsible for the programming of the local church. This is in no way an obstacle; rather, it is an opportunity. If church leaders endorse the start-up of your Spiritual Formation Group—and possibly other groups—you will have taken a major step toward your goal.

If possible, arrange a time when you can sit down and discuss the program with the pastor or priest and other leaders, after they have had a chance to look over your materials. Should they voice concerns or point out potential problems, discuss them thoroughly. They may have small-group plans that do not currently include Spiritual Formation Groups. Try not to leave the meeting before reaching a consensus.

Remember, your task is to get permission to start a Spiritual Formation Group. We have yet to hear of such a request being denied. Most clergy and staff who have become acquainted with the program not only have allowed groups to start but have endorsed them (and sometimes have been involved themselves).

Having gotten permission to begin a group, you are off to a great start. Of course, if you are starting a group not affiliated with a church, you can skip this step and go directly to the next one.

Find One Other Person

The next step is to find at least one other person who wants to form a group. Perhaps you have a close friend, a person at your church who might like to be in a group of this kind. Arrange a time to explain the Spiritual Formation Group and answer any questions (see "The First Meeting" and "Basic Answers to Basic Questions," below). The general rule is this: be enthusiastic but not pushy. Your eagerness to start a group is invaluable. A positive attitude is infectious, and others will be drawn by your excitement alone. But keep in mind that the group will not be for everyone. At this point you are looking for a person who wants to be a part of a group that will challenge him or her.

Once you have found a partner, you have actually established a group. Although many Spiritual Formation Groups involve only two people, you may wish to include others—perhaps friends drawn by your excitement or people who are merely curious. Keep in mind, however, that not everyone will feel comfortable in a Spiritual Formation Group. Do not be surprised if ultimately some participants choose not to commit to the group. If you want to invite others, go on to the next step.

Invite Others to Join You

Do you know other people who would like to be in a Spiritual Formation Group? We have learned through experience that many people would like to be in this kind of small group but have never been invited. The following approaches are effective in finding people who are interested:

*   *Put an announcement in the church newsletter and/or bulletin.*
    Ask the pastoral staff if you may put a notice in the next issue of the church newsletter and/or in the bulletin. Feel free to use the following wording as a guide:

    Are you interested in experiencing growth in your spiritual life? If so, a Spiritual Formation Group will begin meeting on [date] at [time] in [place]. Please call [name] at the church office ([telephone number]) or [name] at [location] ([telephone number]) if you want to join us.

    Be sure to get permission from personnel in the church office before directing telephone calls to them, and tell them what information you need from callers.

*   *Make an announcement during worship.*
    Ask your pastor or priest if you can make a brief announcement during the worship service. People like to see and hear from the person starting a new effort. Alternatively, pastoral leaders can make

the announcement, creating enthusiasm through their obvious support. The announcement can be as short as the above news item, or you can offer more details. Ask people who have questions or are interested in joining the Spiritual Formation Group to meet with you at a specific place in the church (or perhaps at a restaurant) after the service.

- *Send letters and follow up with a telephone call.*
  You can send letters of explanation/invitation to members of your local church, to friends who are not members, or to both groups. Ask God to guide you to the right people. It is more important that each person hunger for the loving accountability provided by a Spiritual Formation Group than that he or she have other interests in common. After you are sure the letters have been received, follow up with a phone call to respond to any questions people may have.

If you are uncomfortable with the above suggestions or are not quite sure if you are ready to start a group larger than two people, you may want to include only yourself and your friend for now. Since this is your group, you can decide whom to meet with, where to meet, and when to begin. But like other decisions about the spiritual life, this one should be made only after careful, thoughtful prayer.

Find the Right Number

How many people should be in a Spiritual Formation Group? We recommend two to seven, though some groups with as many as eight members meet successfully.

The primary reason we recommend limiting the group to seven people is that you will need to be sensitive to how long each meeting lasts. Our experience has shown that when there are too many people in a group, either the group goes beyond the recommended time of one and one-half hours or some members do not have an opportunity to share.

In addition, the level of intimacy decreases when groups become too large. People tend not to share in groups larger than six or seven. They may feel that their participation burdens other group members or that they are using time other members could use better. A group composed of four to five people feels safer for most of us.

Once your group starts, others will hear about it, and eventually more people may wish to join. Feel free to make room for more. Should the Spiritual Formation Group initially be too big or later become too large, you and the other members may decide to divide into two or more smaller groups. If your group is affiliated with a church, your pastoral leaders may want to be involved in the decision to form an additional group.

THE FIRST MEETING: ANSWERING
START-UP QUESTIONS

Once you have advertised the meeting and have enough interested people, you will need to make calls to remind everyone of the time and place. With all of the organization done, you will then be ready for the first meeting.

At that meeting, you will need to give a brief description of what the group will be like and what will be asked of its members (if you have not already done so while talking with people about coming to the first meeting). Other than you and your partner (who, we assume, has a fairly clear idea of what the Spiritual Formation Group will be doing), the other members will probably have some questions. Questions commonly asked include the following:

QUESTION: What is a Spiritual Formation Group?

ANSWER: Most of us want to know in very simple terms what a group we will be meeting with several times is going to be like, what it will try to accomplish, and how it will go about reaching its goal. You will be able to answer these questions by reading over the materials and by becoming familiar with the RENOVARÉ Spiritual Formation Group plan presented in this workbook. This should prepare you to give a succinct explanation of the aim and purpose of your group.

QUESTION: What kind of commitment is expected of me?

ANSWER: An eight-session "test-drive" plus one regular meeting. Share with the others that this is only a trial period during which they will explore a new approach to spiritual formation. The only commitment they are being asked to make is to meet nine times, preferably weekly, for an hour to an hour and a half. The workbook will refer to meetings as *weekly*, but the schedule should be something that is agreeable to all participants.

At the end of the ninth meeting (or, if the group prefers, at a special tenth meeting), the group will evaluate their experience and decide whether or not to continue gathering. This timeframe will help people who are not ready to make a lengthy commitment at the outset. Most of us like to test the water before diving in. After nine meetings the benefits—as well as the work involved—will be apparent. A responsible decision to commit to the group can then be made by each individual.

QUESTION: What will we need to bring with us to the meetings?

ANSWER: We recommend that each person have a copy of this workbook so that the group can proceed through the eight beginning sessions together. You may want to have workbooks available at the first meeting or get them to the members ahead of time. (See page 105 for purchasing and ordering information.)

In addition, the following information may be shared with the group:

During the next nine meetings we will be introduced to six dimensions of Christian discipleship—prayer, virtue, empowerment, compassion, proclamation, and wholeness—as seen in the life of Jesus Christ. We will also learn how we can practice the spiritual disciplines that flow from his life and, between each meeting, do at least one of them on our own. We will gather together and discuss our experiences, thereby learning what it means to encourage one another in our individual spiritual growth.

This is a simplified explanation of the nature and purpose of a Spiritual Formation Group, of course. Feel free to modify, add to, or subtract from the above statement or to take a different approach altogether.

BASIC ANSWERS TO BASIC QUESTIONS

You may want to discuss the following questions with all participants before you meet with the group the first time, or you may want to take a few moments at the beginning of the first meeting to address them. If you choose the latter approach, ask each member to read the Introduction in this workbook before the first meeting. It may not answer all of their questions, but it will give them a sense of the nature of the group.

With that groundwork, your group will be ready to begin the first session!

QUESTION: Should groups be composed of only men or only women, or can they be mixed?

ANSWER: That will be up to you. We have learned that the level of intimacy and sharing is much deeper and develops much more quickly if group members are the same gender. Why? The more a group of people has in common, the more they can relate to each other. They share similar struggles and talk about them with fewer inhibitions. And yet there is something to be said in favor of a mixed group, with its added variety, broader spectrum of life experiences, and differing perspectives. The makeup of the group is ultimately up to you.

QUESTION: Can husbands and wives be in the same group?

ANSWER: Yes. But many groups that include husbands and wives report that participating together is a mixed blessing. On the one hand, it can be a tremendous way for a couple to grow closer, and it adds incentives in the area of mutual accountability. On the other hand, some people report struggling over what they should or should not share. Spouses sometimes hesitate to share a private struggle, feeling that they should try to work it out on their own, thus preventing them from benefiting from the help of the group.

On the other hand, numerous couples form a Spiritual Formation Group by themselves. They meet regularly with each other to review how they are doing and to make plans for the future, sharing their joys and concerns with one another. Whether husbands and wives should be in the same group with other people or with each other depends upon what the individuals find the most beneficial.

QUESTION: Is a Spiritual Formation Group for "saints" only?

ANSWER: No. While the title may sound a bit ominous, Spiritual Formation Groups are designed to meet the needs of people who have little knowledge of the spiritual disciplines and minimal experience doing them. The workbook uses a step-by-step approach to teach and model the disciplines, explaining the "whats" and "whys" and especially the "hows."

Does this mean that the workbook is too easy for the more spiritually mature? No. The exercises that you will do are basic and foundational and meet you where you are. At the same time, they challenge you to move ahead, to grow spiritually.

QUESTION: What can I expect to happen to me in a Spiritual Formation Group?

ANSWER: There is nothing magical about Spiritual Formation Groups. They contain no secret formula and they offer no easy shortcuts. What they do offer is a plan that helps you put yourself in a place where God can transform your life from the inside out.

By providing you with balance (the six dimensions of discipleship), knowledge (the chapter titled "Ideas and Exercises"), and encouragement (the loving accountability), a Spiritual Formation Group can initiate in you a renewed and deepening spiritual life.

With the questions answered, your group is ready to do Session 1 during the next meeting! God bless you in your ongoing efforts to be an effective disciple of Jesus Christ. Always remember that ultimately the work is God's, not ours.

# Eight Beginning Sessions

BECOMING A SPIRITUAL FORMATION GROUP

SESSION ONE

Discovering a Balanced Vision of Christian Faith and Practice

THE LIFE OF JESUS CHRIST

For the leader: After the group has gathered and is ready to begin, ask them to spend a few moments (allow two to five minutes) in silent prayer. When you sense that the time is right, begin the session with Exercise 1.

THE FOOTPRINTS OF GOD
Exercise 1
Jesus Christ functions in four main ways in the Christian's life: Savior, Teacher, Lord, and Friend. In our relationship with him, each of us experiences some of these roles more powerfully than others. Which role have you experienced the most and do you understand the best? In which would you like to see yourself grow stronger?

> *Jesus Christ as my Savior: he forgives my sins and sets me free.*
>
> *Jesus Christ as my Teacher: he teaches me wisdom and guides me into truth.*
>
> *Jesus Christ as my Lord: he lives at the center of my life.*
>
> *Jesus Christ as my Friend: he understands and comforts me.*

Beginning with the leader, answer these questions.

Allow each member a few minutes to respond.

UNDERSTANDING A BALANCED CHRISTIAN LIFE
The previous question reveals two things about us. First, we are often quite familiar with one way God works in our lives. Second, we are often equally unfamiliar with other ways God works in our lives. This should not discourage us. We should be thankful that God has moved in our lives in profound ways. But it should encourage us to build on our strengths as we stretch and grow in other, less familiar, areas.

The leader reads this entire section.

The study you are now beginning will help you identify certain strong, familiar areas in your spiritual life and other weaker, less familiar ones. We all have tendencies, habits, and "comfort zones" where we feel secure and content. When we leave these comfort zones, we may feel anxious and unsettled. Those feelings keep many of us from growing. Authentic spiritual growth requires that we venture out of our comfort zones and experience God in new and exciting ways.

RECOGNIZING OUR STRENGTHS
Exercise 2

Ask everyone to answer this question.

In which of the following areas do you feel most at ease—that is, which are your comfort zones?

> *I love to be at work.*
>
> *I feel comfortable with a group of close friends.*
>
> *I enjoy playing sports.*
>
> *I cherish being at home in my garden or reading.*
>
> *I like to be with large groups of people.*

A PROGRAM FLOWING OUT OF THE LIFE OF JESUS

Have a member of the group read this section.

The RENOVARÉ Spiritual Formation program is based on the life of Jesus Christ. As we look at his life (in Sessions 2 through 7), we will see that he had a full and complete life with God. When we read the Gospels:

> We see Jesus praying, and we listen to his teaching on the life of intimacy with God.
>
> We see Jesus battling with Satan in the wilderness, and we listen to his teaching on the importance of a pure heart.
>
> We see Jesus ministering in great power, and we listen to his teaching on the comfort, wisdom, and strength that come from the Holy Spirit.
>
> We see Jesus helping the sick and the needy, and we listen to his teaching on the importance of caring for our neighbor.
>
> We see Jesus proclaiming the good news of the kingdom of heaven, and we listen to him reading from the Scriptures.
>
> We see Jesus integrating sacred and secular while observing the ceremonies of his faith.

From the life of Jesus Christ there emerge six distinct areas:

> Devotion to God
>
> Virtue in thought, word, and action
>
> Empowerment by the Spirit
>
> Compassion toward all people

Proclamation of the good news of the gospel

Harmony between faith and work

RENOVARÉ Spiritual Formation Groups are rooted in these six areas. The goal is to gain an understanding of these aspects of Jesus' life and incorporate them into our lives daily. By doing so, we will grow more and more Christlike.

Exercise 3
Which areas of Jesus' life are you most familiar with?

The leader asks each person to answer this question.

- *Praying*
- *Striving against sin*
- *Ministering and healing in the power of the Spirit*
- *Showing compassion*
- *Proclaiming the good news and reading the Scriptures*
- *Uniting the physical and spiritual*

SIX MOVEMENTS IN THE HISTORY OF THE CHURCH
The history of the Church has been marked by *movements,* a word used to describe how God's Spirit has moved upon individuals and groups of people with a particular mission. Usually such a movement has emphasized one of the six areas mentioned above—often called the *Six Traditions*—bringing a focused renewal to the Church. When one effort has waned, a new movement stressing another area has emerged. The following examples illustrate one movement in each Tradition:

Choose a member to read this section.

In the fourth century men and women fled city life to found cloisters and monasteries where they emphasized the importance of solitude, meditation, and prayer. Antony of Egypt was an early leader of these "Desert Mothers and Fathers." The Church was strengthened by their emphasis upon intimacy with God, and a *contemplative movement* was born.

In the early eighteenth century John Wesley and his friends formed a group nicknamed the "Holy Club" and began focusing on moral laxity and the need for Christians to overcome sinful habits. They developed a "method," and the Church once again took sin seriously. The purifying effects of the Methodist effort were dramatic, and it became a *holiness movement.*

In the seventeenth century the Church witnessed a new outbreak of the Holy Spirit in the lives of men and women who were called "Quakers," led by the ministry of George Fox. The active presence of the Spirit in the lives of believers became the empowering principle behind scores of conversions. The active role of the Spirit was at the center of their worship, and it propelled them into evangelism, missions, and social concern. This is an example of a *charismatic movement.*

In the late twelfth century Francis of Assisi and a group of followers abandoned their former lives and went about the Italian countryside, caring for the sick, the poor, and the lame. Countless men and women followed Francis's lead, forming the Franciscan and Poor Clare orders. Their impact on disease and poverty was remarkable, and they became an example of a *social justice movement.*

In the sixteenth century Martin Luther and others proclaimed the gospel of Jesus Christ after discovering its message anew in the Bible. This message of hope and victory was expressed by clergy and laity in sermons, mission efforts, and personal witnessing. In the history of the Church it is a wonderful example of an *evangelical movement.*

In the eighteenth century Count Nikolaus Ludwig von Zinzendorf allowed remnants of the persecuted Moravian Church (Unitas Fratum) to build the village of Herrnhut on his estate. Initially divided, the group became unified when they experienced a powerful outpouring of the Holy Spirit after Zinzendorf led them in daily Bible studies and in formulating the "Brotherly Agreement." The Moravians joyfully served God—praying, evangelizing, and helping others—in the midst of baking, teaching, weaving, and raising families. This is an example of an *incarnational movement.*

There have been other similar movements, both before and after the examples mentioned above, but certainly these stand out as efforts that have had particularly dramatic effects upon the life and history of the Church.

MOVEMENTS AND THE LIFE OF CHRIST
Exercise 4

Beginning with the leader, complete this exercise.

Each of the above movements began with an emphasis on one of the aspects of the life of Jesus Christ. Match the aspect of Jesus' life with the corresponding Tradition:

1. *Compassion toward all people*
2. *Devotion to God*
3. *Proclamation of the good news of the gospel*
4. *Empowerment by the Spirit*
5. *Harmony between faith and work*
6. *Virtue in thought, word, and action*

A. *The holiness movement*
B. *The charismatic movement*
C. *The contemplative movement*
D. *The evangelical movement*
E. *The social justice movement*
F. *The incarnational movement*

(Answers: 1-E; 2-C; 3-D; 4-B; 5-F; 6-A)

GIVEN TO EXTREMES

Exercise 5

While each of the movements described above (and others like them in the Six Traditions) was rooted in the life of Christ, as "movements" they were sometimes given to extremes. Within each one there were adherents who overemphasized their particular area of strength. That lack of balance is still common in the Church today. We see, for example,

Ask one of the members to read this section.

> The contemplative who fails to do creative work
>
> The moralist who focuses on sin and neglects compassion
>
> The charismatic who neglects to proclaim the gospel
>
> The social activist who forgets to listen to God
>
> The evangelist who feels no need for the Holy Spirit
>
> The schoolteacher who revels in secret, harmful sins

Since you have been a Christian, which of these extremes have you seen most?

Beginning with the person who read the material in Exercise 5, answer this question.

The problems that we have been discussing may lead us to avoid a certain area; however, we really do need all of the Six Traditions functioning in our lives. One area without the others—or one that dominates the others—will naturally lead to divisive and harmful extremes.

Once discussion has ended, the leader reads this paragraph.

IDENTIFYING OUR STRENGTHS AND WEAKNESSES

Exercise 6

Looking over the Six Traditions of the Church—the varied dimensions of the spiritual life—and thinking about movements that represent them, identify the area that you would consider to be your greatest strength. Which comes the most naturally? Which would you consider your weakest?

The leader explains the exercise and asks the questions.

The dimensions of the spiritual life are much like a wheel. A wheel is formed by placing spokes around a center hub. Each spoke must be equally strong and equally long in order for the wheel to function properly. If any spoke is too short, the wheel may still roll, but it will thump distinctly with the effort, not functioning as it should. We, too, will go "bump, bump" in our spiritual lives if one area is stronger or longer than another.

Below is a diagram of the Six Traditions, arranged around the spokes of a wheel. Take a few moments and, using a scale of 1 to 10 (with 1 being the least proficient and closest to the center of the wheel), estimate where you are in each area on the wheel spokes. Place dots at those points; then connect the dots from spoke to spoke to form a ring around the hub.

Pause to give everyone a chance to fill out the diagram. Then, beginning with someone who has not begun a discussion, ask all members to share what they feel are their weakest and strongest areas by answering the above questions.

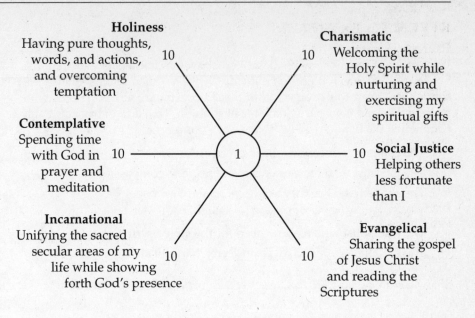

Holiness
Having pure thoughts, words, and actions, and overcoming temptation

Charismatic
Welcoming the Holy Spirit while nurturing and exercising my spiritual gifts

Contemplative
Spending time with God in prayer and meditation

Social Justice
Helping others less fortunate than I

Incarnational
Unifying the sacred secular areas of my life while showing forth God's presence

Evangelical
Sharing the gospel of Jesus Christ and reading the Scriptures

At the end of the discussion, ask these questions.

How many feel that your "wheel" goes bump, bump? What does that bumping make you want to do?

REJOICE IN WHAT YOU HAVE, WHAT YOU WILL HAVE, AND WHAT OTHERS HAVE

After everyone has had a chance to share, the leader reads this section.

Our discussion reveals that some of us are strong in some areas or Traditions where others are not, and vice versa. This gives us some important insights. First, we have a lot for which we can thank God. God has touched each of our lives in some important ways and has given us unique abilities and talents. We are strong in particular areas so that we can exercise those gifts as a part of our ministry to the Church. We should rejoice in these strengths.

Second, we have a lot of room to grow. But do not be discouraged! It is extremely rare to find a person who is strong in all six areas. The challenge and excitement of this program come when we start becoming strong in areas that we previously saw as impossible. As we look at the above exercise, we should experience hope; growth in these areas is right around the corner for each of us. Let us rejoice in what God will do in the coming weeks.

Third, very seldom do all the members of a group share exactly the same strengths and weaknesses. This is one of the great benefits of being in a group: we build upon each other's strengths. When you hear people say that they are strong in areas in which you are not, be thankful for what God has given them. In addition, thank God that they are in the group with you, for their strengths will help build you up. Rejoice in the strengths God has given each person.

REFLECTING ON GOD'S PRESENCE

Sometime during the coming week, take a few minutes to write a brief "letter to God." In this letter, try to recall the first time you sensed God's presence and some of the ways God has revealed himself to you since then. Close the letter by giving thanks for all that you know of God now and for all that you would like to know in the future. The letter should be about one page in length, and it will be shared (if you choose) at the beginning of the next week's gathering.

The leader reads this section.

ENDING AND BEGINNING

Exercise 7

Passing the Peace: Each member speaks a word of encouragement to other members individually, mentioning gratefully what God has done in their lives. For example, "Bill, I want to encourage you in your ability to help others, and I thank God for what he has done and continues to do in your life."

Allow a few minutes for each member of the group to participate in this exercise.

A WONDERFUL JOURNEY AWAITS YOU

In the next seven sessions we will delve more deeply into the six areas (or Traditions) that we have been discussing. In each session not only will we learn about these Traditions, but we will also discover some simple ways in which we can begin working their accompanying disciplines into our lives.

Go now with the grace and peace of God. Let us close by joining hands and praying the Lord's Prayer aloud and in unison.

After the peace has been passed, the leader reads this section.

Our Father, who art in heaven,
Hallowed be thy name.
Thy kingdom come,
Thy will be done,
On earth as it is in heaven.
Give us this day our daily bread;
And forgive us our trespasses
As we forgive those who trespass against us.
And lead us not into temptation,
But deliver us from evil.
For thine is the kingdom, and the power, and the glory, forever and ever.
Amen.

All members join hands in a circle and pray the Lord's Prayer aloud and in unison.

Ask for a volunteer to lead the next meeting.

Practicing the Prayer-Filled Life

THE CONTEMPLATIVE TRADITION

THE FOOTPRINTS OF GOD

After a few minutes of silent prayer, open with a time of sharing that the leader begins by reading this opening paragraph, sharing his or her "letter to God," and answering the question posed.

At our last meeting each of us agreed to write a short "letter to God." I will read my letter aloud first and answer the question, *What did I learn about God and about myself from doing this exercise?* After I have finished, please take turns reading your letter to us and answering the same question.

JESUS AND THE PRAYER-FILLED LIFE

Gospel Passage: Mark 14:32–36

When everyone has had a chance to respond, ask a member to read this Scripture passage.

They went to a place called Gethsemane; and [Jesus] said to his disciples, "Sit here while I pray." He took with him Peter and James and John, and began to be distressed and agitated. And said to them, "I am deeply grieved, even to death; remain here, and keep awake." And going a little farther, he threw himself on the ground and prayed that, if it were possible, the hour might pass from him. He said, "Abba, Father, for you all things are possible; remove this cup from me; yet, not what I want, but what you want."

Reflection Question

What impresses you the most about this passage?

THINKING IT THROUGH

After a brief discussion, choose someone to read this section.

Jesus was a very busy person, yet in this passage, as in many others, we see that he took time to talk with God (Mark 1:35, 6:46; Matt. 14:22–23a; Luke 6:12). One might easily conclude from reading the Gospels that the central focus of Jesus' life was his relationship with the Father. He said that he could do nothing apart from God and that his entire mission in life was to do the will of God (John 5:19). We see this focus in Jesus' daily life. He frequently left the crowds to be alone with God, retreating to "a deserted place" to pray (Mark 1:35). He became a role model for the disciples; when they looked at Jesus, they longed to be like him, to have the same kind of intimacy with God that he had. That is why they said, "Lord, teach us to pray" (Luke 11:1). The disciples knew that Jesus knew how to pray.

What set Jesus apart from the disciples was the intimate relationship he had with the Father. Notice how he addressed God: "Abba, Father." The word "Abba" is similar to our word "Daddy." It indicates closeness, love, a trusting relationship like that of little children to their parents. Jesus was not afraid to talk with God, to share his fears and his anguish. In the Garden of Gethsemane—at his moment of greatest need—Jesus prayed. His prayer was faith-full: "For you all things are possible." His prayer was honest: "Remove this cup from me." And in the end his prayer expressed a desire to do the will of God: "Yet, not what I want, but what you want."

Jesus was a person of prayer. He prayed regularly; he prayed often. The busier he got, the more he talked with God. Why? Because he *knew* God! He knew God as "Abba," his loving Father, whose main interest was to love, to teach, and to heal his people. For Jesus, God was not only a God of compassion but also a God of strength. Jesus turned to God to find the strength he needed to complete his task. By his actions, Jesus became a model, a "divine paradigm" that we can imitate.

Jesus asked God to "remove the cup" from him—the cup symbolizing his destiny to die on the Cross. Why do you think he prayed this way?

Reflection Question

GOD AND THE CONTEMPLATIVE TRADITION

At the heart of each Tradition of the Church is God. Jesus is "God with us," a physical presence to show us what God is like. His actions and words reveal God's nature to us. When we practice "the prayer-filled life"—that is, the Contemplative Tradition—we discover the tender love of God. Jesus prays to the Father because he knows God's nature—loving, giving, forgiving. Jesus tells us that God knows our needs even before we ask him (Matt. 6:8). Jesus describes (and demonstrates in his own life) a God of compassion and long-suffering love who desires to bless us with wisdom and courage and inner healing.

Have one member of the group read this entire section.

The most vivid picture of God's tender love comes in the story of the Prodigal Son (Luke 15:11–32). A wayward son who has squandered his father's money—his own inheritance—returns in repentance and remorse, expecting judgment and punishment. Instead he receives a loving welcome and a warm embrace. This is God's nature, what he is like. If we knew God in this way—as a loving, forgiving Father—praying and talking with him would not be a chore or a duty but would rather be our inner desire throughout the day. God longs for us, searches for us—and even died for us—in hopes that we will respond to his longing, searching, self-sacrificing love. Once we catch a glimpse of what God is like, we will want to spend time with him.

Reflection Question
Allow each person a few moments to respond to this question.

As before, have a member read this entire section.

The father in the story of the Prodigal Son gives us a snapshot of the nature of God. How does this picture match your own understanding of what God is like?

WHAT IS THE CONTEMPLATIVE TRADITION?

From Jesus we see, hear, and learn about God's nature. Because he knew what God is like, Jesus—as we have seen—frequently spent time with him in solitude and in prayer. These two factors—the nature of God and the practice of Jesus—gave birth to the Contemplative Tradition.

The Contemplative Tradition is a response to God's longing that we spend time with him, that we create space in our lives to be with him. Our lives are busy and full of worries and anxiety, and our usual response is to push God out of the way entirely. Practicing the disciplines of the Contemplative Tradition equips us to create in our lives the "space" that God longs for and the intimacy that we need.

Most of us live in the midst of jobs and families and responsibilities that hamper our efforts to spend time with God. And everything in our hurry-scurry culture works against our efforts to set aside time for him. Colleges and businesses provide courses in time management so that we can squeeze every drop from every minute. Televisions bombard us with ads that tempt us to spend our "leisure time" shopping or attending movies or eating out. Radios incessantly broadcast talk shows, music, sports events, and news analyses with such force that the sound vibrates our inner organs. Sometimes even our backgrounds prompt us to feel guilty when we are not doing something "creative."

We all agree that it is *very* difficult to make space for God in our day and in our culture, and yet we need times of solitude and silence, times of contemplation and reflection, times of prayer and meditation. We need these times—just as much as Jesus needed them—to gain strength and wisdom and compassion. All three qualities flow from the space we make for God in our lives.

Reflection Question
Give each member a chance to respond to this question if he or she wishes.

Think of a moment in your life when you felt very close to God. Can you describe the setting (what you were doing and your surroundings) as well as the experience?

PRACTICING THE CONTEMPLATIVE TRADITION

We have looked at the practice of Jesus, the nature of God, and the main goal of the Contemplative Tradition. Now we turn our attention to the actual practice of that Tradition. The following list includes activities by which we can begin to enter the "prayer-filled life," a life of intimacy with God. These "spiritual disciplines" or "spiritual exercises" help open us to God's presence. Each exercise is followed by a brief explanation of how to do it. Choose *one* of the following exercises and practice it several times before the next meeting. Why? Because experience is the best teacher. You are trying to become "full of prayer," and to become prayer-full, you have to pray. Keep in mind that these are only a sampling of many exercises that can help you enter into the contemplative life.

Again, choose a member to read these paragraphs.

Three simple precautions: First, do not be afraid to fail. To reach a goal is not the reason you do a spiritual discipline; it is to experience God. Even in failure you are learning and experiencing new and valuable things. Second, keep your emphasis on God, not on the method. It is hard initially, but try to think about *why* you are doing an exercise rather than *what* you are doing. Third, feel free to modify any exercise to fit your needs. In the first session we looked at our areas of strength and weakness. You may be strong in this area—the prayer-filled life—or you may be weak. Adapt the exercise you choose to challenge your strengths and support your weaknesses.

EXERCISES IN THE CONTEMPLATIVE TRADITION

1. *Set aside five to ten minutes each day for prayer.*
    Find a time in your schedule that is free of interruption, when you can turn your thoughts to God. You may want to read a Bible verse and meditate on it, or you may want to spend the time talking with God about your needs and concerns. The idea is simply to set aside your busy activities (or not start them) and turn your attention to God.

Have each member read over the exercises silently, or have members read them aloud, one at a time. Spend a few moments considering them as each person chooses the exercise he or she will do before the next meeting.

2. *Spend five to ten minutes each day in silence.*
    Carve out a time that is free from interruption and use this time to be silent. While letting silence and its peace wash over you, pray without words. Very close friends can communicate without words; try this with God. Simply enjoy God's presence, God's loving arms wrapped around you.

3. *Read selections from a devotional book.*
    Find a book on the spiritual life that interests you. It may be a spiritual classic such as St. Augustine's *Confessions,* or it may be a devotional classic such as Oswald Chambers's *My Utmost for His Highest.* Devotional periodicals such as *Guideposts* or *The Upper Room* (or some other denominational publication) may interest you. However, instead of reading what you select simply to understand it, read it "with God," knowing that God is there in the room with you. Discover God in the reading.

4. *Pray the same prayer for ten minutes each day.*
    There is a tradition in the Eastern Church called "hesychasm," which is the practice of repeating a simple prayer over and over. The idea is to focus our thoughts on God so that God can enter our heart. You might like to try the "hesychastic" prayer "Lord Jesus Christ, Son of God, have mercy on me," or use a verse from a psalm—perhaps "Create in me a clean heart, O God" (Ps. 51:10).

5. *Write an original prayer.*
    Take time to write a prayer as if it were a "letter to God." Beginning with "Dear God," tell God your hopes and dreams, your worries, your needs. You may even want to confess your sins and ask for forgiveness. Most important, use the prayer to open the lines of communication between yourself and God. Do not write the prayer as though it would be read by others someday. Like a personal journal, keep your prayer confidential so that you have the freedom to be honest. Once you are done, read and pray it every day until our next gathering.

ENDING AND BEGINNING

Allow each member time to share which of the above exercises he or she plans to do during the week. Encourage each other in this venture. After everyone has shared, join hands in a circle and pray the Lord's Prayer aloud and in unison.

Ask for a volunteer to lead the next meeting.

Our Father, who art in heaven,
Hallowed be thy name.
Thy kingdom come,
Thy will be done,
On earth as it is in heaven.
Give us this day our daily bread;
And forgive us our trespasses
As we forgive those who trespass against us.
And lead us not into temptation,
But deliver us from evil.
For thine is the kingdom, and the power, and the glory, forever and ever.
Amen.

SESSION THREE
Practicing the Virtuous Life

THE HOLINESS TRADITION

THE FOOTPRINTS OF GOD

At our last meeting each of us agreed to try one of the exercises in the Contemplative Tradition. Let's share our experiences by answering the following question:

What did you learn about God and about yourself while doing the exercise?

After a few minutes of silent prayer, open with a time of sharing that the leader begins by reading this opening paragraph and answering the question posed.

JESUS AND THE VIRTUOUS LIFE

Gospel Passage: Matthew 4:1–11

Then Jesus was led up by the Spirit into the wilderness to be tempted by the devil. He fasted forty days and forty nights, and afterwards he was famished. The tempter came and said to him, "If you are the Son of God, command these stones to become loaves of bread." But he answered, "It is written,

'One does not live by bread alone,
but by every word that comes from the mouth of God.'"

Then the devil took him to the holy city and placed him on the pinnacle of the temple, saying to him, "If you are the Son of God, throw yourself down; for it is written,

'He will command his angels concerning you,'
and 'On their hands they will bear you up,
so that you will not dash your foot against a stone.'"

When everyone has had a chance to respond, ask a member to read this Scripture passage.

Jesus said to him, "Again it is written, 'Do not put the Lord your God to the test.'"

Again, the devil took him to a very high mountain and showed him all the kingdoms of the world and their splendor; and he said to him, "All these I will give you, if you will fall down and worship me." Jesus said to him, "Away with you, Satan! for it is written,

'Worship the Lord your God, and serve only him.'"

Then the devil left him, and suddenly angels came and waited on him.

Reflection Question

Have you ever had someone come to you and tempt you with an offer that was hard to refuse? Describe the circumstances.

THINKING IT THROUGH

After a brief discussion, choose someone to read this section.

Jesus' baptism comes right before his testing in the wilderness (Matt. 3:13–17). This is important, because at the conclusion of his baptism a "voice from heaven" proclaims that Jesus is "his Son" (Matt. 3:17). Exactly who Jesus is has just been confirmed, and now the devil will do everything he can to destroy Jesus.

Notice that it was "the Spirit" who led Jesus into the wilderness "to be tempted." This may seem odd to us: How could God instigate Jesus' temptation? The word translated "to be tempted" actually means "to be tested." There is a subtle but important difference. God tests; the devil tempts. God does not want Jesus to fail; the devil does. The Spirit leads Jesus into the wilderness to fast and to pray and to resist the forces that assault him during his mission. Having overcome them, he is ready for his journey toward the Cross.

There are three temptations: turn stones into bread, leap off the temple roof to see if angels will come to the rescue, and acquire all of the kingdoms in the world. The first two temptations challenge Jesus to prove his deity: "If you are the Son of God . . . "; the last temptation dares Jesus to reject his deity. Jesus rebukes all three by quoting from the Hebrew Scriptures (Deut. 8:3; 6:16; 6:13). The devil shows that he too knows the Scriptures, trying to make the second temptation more appealing by quoting from Psalm 91 (vss. 11–12). However, Jesus knows better, and he cannot be tricked. In the end the devil leaves because he has been unable to entice Jesus to sin.

It is important for us to see one thing: Jesus remained true to his mission throughout his testing and emerged pure at its end. He could have turned stones into bread—he had the power. He knew that God would protect him—he had the relationship. He could have accepted the devil's offer of power and fame and glory—a much more pleasant destiny than execution on a cross. But he did not; three times Jesus did not yield. His responses tell us much about the nature of sin and the importance of purity.

Reflection Question

Why did Jesus not yield to any of these temptations?

GOD AND THE HOLINESS TRADITION

God cares about sin. The Bible makes it very clear that the people of God can be free from the power of sin. And what is sin? According to the Bible sin is rejecting the commandments of God. Adam and Eve rejected God's command and ate the fruit; the people of Israel rejected God's command and fashioned a golden calf; Jonah rejected God's command and ran away from his calling. Every time the commands of God were rejected in the scriptural narrative, disaster followed. Disaster still trails the heels of sin. Why follow God's commands? Because God knows the consequences of sin.

Have one member of the group read this entire section.

Most of us are accustomed to thinking of God's commandments as rules that stifle our happiness and make us feel guilty. How untrue this notion is! The commands of God are given to us so that we might live abundantly. Take, for example, the Ten Commandments (Exod. 20:2–17). Each commandment calls us to the blessed life, the pathway to true happiness. The seventh commandment, "You shall not commit adultery," may seem to restrict our sexual freedom. In reality, though, the opposite is true. To engage in an adulterous affair leads to pain and loneliness; to remain faithful to our spouse brings true freedom. God knows this.

Holiness is something God wishes for us simply because it is the best way to live. The commandments of God are not meant to make our lives a dull drudgery, but to make them whole and full. God's plan completes and integrates our lives; sin disrupts and fragments our lives. While sin seems appealing on the surface—the fulfillment of all of our desires—beneath the surface lurks poison that will ultimately destroy us.

Writer and philosopher Dallas Willard teaches that sin is "slop." Sin stains and ruins our souls. We are drawn to it and tempted by its whispers of pleasure only to find that it offers a short season of delight and a long— sometimes lifelong—season of pain. Because God knows this, he prescribes a way of living that helps us resist the seductive yet destructive clutches of sin. Living a holy life is not limited to "super saints"; rather, it is healthy and functional for everyone.

How have you seen disobeying one of God's commands or the power of sin fragment and destroy a person's life?

Reflection Question
Allow each person a few moments to respond to this question.

WHAT IS THE HOLINESS TRADITION?

From the heart of God and the manifest life of Jesus, we have seen how God desires holiness, purity, and virtue in our lives. A holy life has been defined as a life that is functional and healthy and whole. But holiness, or purity of heart, is not merely obedience to certain rules. Jesus chastened the Pharisees for outwardly obeying God's law while neglecting the "word of God"—that is, the spirit of the law.

As before, have a member read this entire section.

Holiness was defined by the Israelites as a way to separate the clean from the unclean. Later, the Pharisees in particular refined the definitions of holiness in terms of outward rituals that determined "clean" and "unclean." Washing properly, not working on the Sabbath, eating only certain foods, avoiding the company of Gentiles (especially tax collectors and harlots)—all these were the way to holiness. But Jesus openly challenged this division between inward purity and outward ritual. "What goes into your mouth does not make you 'unclean,' but what comes out of your mouth, that is what makes you 'unclean'" (Matt. 15:11, NIV). Jesus turns our attention away from ritual purity and points to the purity of heart from which flows unshakable obedience to God (Matt. 5:8).

Yet Jesus also said, "If you wish to enter into life, keep the commandments" (Matt. 19:17). Not keeping the commandments is not even an option. We do not refer to them as the "Ten Suggestions," as if they were hints to help us improve ourselves. No, keeping the commandments is mandatory, and God provides a way to obey them: yielding our lives to him. Obedience is the natural outgrowth of a life that is bound to God. If we are in love with God, we will obey his laws. Why? Because we love and trust God as a child loves and trusts a parent. Thus we follow his way. We do not obey his commands grudgingly; rather, we keep them willingly, because our experience with God proves that obeying his commands is our best course of action. To trust and obey is at the heart of the Holiness Tradition. As we shall see, trusting and obeying manifest themselves in our lives in many ways.

Reflection Question
Give each member a chance to respond to this question if he or she wishes.

Why did Jesus criticize the Pharisees for focusing on outward action rather than on the inner source of action?

PRACTICING THE HOLINESS TRADITION

Again, choose a member to read these paragraphs.

Once again we have come to a place where our theology must become practical. Since God desires for us to be holy, it is our task to find ways to enter into his way of holiness.

We have noted that it is not merely outward obedience of certain rules or rituals that makes us holy. When we engage in certain disciplines, we are not instantly holy, nor have we completed a task that is rewarded by a merit badge of godliness. Rather, we do certain disciplines and exercises as a means of training, much as an athlete trains to become more proficient at a particular sport.

The result of doing the following exercises is a greater ability to obey God's commandments. We become able to do that which we were unable to do, able to keep commandments we were unable to keep. For example, two of the following exercises help discipline the tongue. If I tell myself simply to stop saying negative things, I will likely fail. But if I begin with the "inside"—praying for a pure heart and then committing to watch my words—I open the door to the Spirit to begin helping me. When I am about to say something negative, the Spirit speaks a word of caution to me, and that blessed split second makes change in my behavior possible.

The result is not, "Wow, aren't I special because I stopped saying negative things!" (which sounds much like the words of the Pharisee in Jesus' parable in Luke 18:9–14), but rather, "God is beginning to mold and shape my life." Remembering the difference between working from the inside out and from the outside in is extremely important when practicing these disciplines.

EXERCISES IN THE HOLINESS TRADITION

1. *Pray for the Holy Spirit to purify your heart and mind; then listen.*
   In bringing about change, God works from the inside out and he works via the Holy Spirit. Set aside a substantial amount of time (say, one hour) for a deep and heartfelt prayer. During that time, ask God to purify your heart and mind through the power of the Holy Spirit. The key to the effectiveness of your prayer will be your willingness to surrender control of your life to God. Ask God to search your heart to see if there is any hidden evil in your life or any activity that God wants you to quit. Then listen. When you have a sense of what God wants to free you from, pray that the Spirit will purge that sin—even the desire for it—from your life. Holiness is born in prayers like these.

   Have each member read over the exercises silently, or have members read them aloud, one at a time. Spend a few moments considering them as each person chooses the exercise he or she will do before the next meeting.

2. *Respond to temptation with the word of God.*
   Jesus overcame the devil's temptations by holding fast to God's commandments. Memorize those three responses (Deut. 8:3; 6:16; 6:13), and when you are tempted by the enemy to (1) gratify selfish desires, (2) doubt God's power, or (3) seek wealth, power, or fame, respond to the temptation with the corresponding verse of Scripture. Jesus used the power of God through Scripture to defeat the devil, and so can we.

3. *Try a twenty-four-hour partial fast.*
   Jesus fasted in the wilderness to gain spiritual strength. When we fast, we are saying no to the uncontrolled appetites of our body and thereby gaining mastery over them. The practice of fasting also reveals hidden traits—anger, selfishness, inability to delay gratification, laziness, and so on—which can become areas for change (and growth) in the future. A simple way to begin is to fast from lunch to lunch, skipping dinner and breakfast in between. After eating lunch on the first day, do not eat a full meal until lunch on the second day. During the twenty-four hours drink plenty of water, and at mealtimes drink a glass of fruit juice if you want. Remember, in the fasting you are "feasting" upon God.

4. *Practice these two disciplines for "taming the tongue."*
   What we say reveals what is in our hearts. That is why Jesus said that it is not what goes into the mouth but what comes out that defiles a

person (Matt. 15:11). In other words, what we say makes us "unclean." James also reminds us of the power of words (James 3:5–12). Like fire, they can refine or destroy. The following disciplines will help you monitor the things you say and gain some control over the awesome power of the tongue.

- *Go a day without saying anything negative.*
  In the morning, ask the Holy Spirit to "set a guard over [your] mouth" (Ps. 141:3), preventing you from saying anything negative. Be ruthless about this! Do not let even the slightest hint of criticism or judgment come out of your mouth. You may find yourself in situations that call for an honest appraisal; for example, you may be asked what you think about something. Be honest, but do not be critical. Instead, search for ways to be positive about everything around you and be ready to give compliments as often as you can.

- *Go a day without saying anything that is dishonest.*
  Jesus said of Nathaniel that he was a person without "guile" (John 1:47, KJV). What a compliment! Guile is dishonesty, deceit, double-talk, falsehood, shading the truth, manipulating words, and the like. Pray that the Spirit will make your heart pure and honest and alert you to anything that is less than forthright. Do not manipulate your words; let your "yes" be "yes" and your "no" be "no."

In both of these activities you will find a great sense of release. Our negative words hurt not only others but ourselves as well; they affect our spirit. The old adage says, "When we throw mud, we can't help but get some on ourselves." When we say dishonest things, we live in fear that we will be found out, that someone will see through our falsehood. We are forced to tell more lies to keep the original lie going. We find freedom and peace when we begin taming the tongue.

ENDING AND BEGINNING

Our Father, who art in heaven,
Hallowed be thy name.
Thy kingdom come,
Thy will be done,
On earth as it is in heaven.
Give us this day our daily bread;
And forgive us our trespasses
As we forgive those who trespass against us.
And lead us not into temptation,
But deliver us from evil.
For thine is the kingdom, and the power, and the glory, forever and ever.
Amen.

Allow each member time to share which of the above exercises he or she plans to do during the week. Encourage each other in this venture. After everyone has shared, join hands in a circle and pray the Lord's Prayer aloud and in unison.

Ask for a volunteer to lead the next meeting.

SESSION FOUR

Practicing the Spirit-Empowered Life

THE CHARISMATIC TRADITION

THE FOOTPRINTS OF GOD

After a few minutes of silent prayer, open with a time of sharing that the leader begins by reading this opening paragraph and answering the question posed.

At our last meeting each of us agreed to try one of the exercises in the Holiness Tradition. Let's share our experiences by answering the following question:

What did you learn about God and about yourself while doing the exercise?

JESUS AND THE SPIRIT-EMPOWERED LIFE
Gospel Passage: John 14:15–17, 25–26; 15:26–27; 16:7–15

When everyone has had a chance to respond, ask a member to read this Scripture passage.

"If you love me, you will keep my commandments. And I will ask the Father, and he will give you another Advocate, to be with you forever. This is the Spirit of truth, whom the world cannot receive, because it neither sees him nor knows him. You know him, because he abides with you, and he will be in you. . . .

"I have said these things to you while I am still with you. But the Advocate, the Holy Spirit, whom the Father will send in my name, will teach you everything, and remind you of all that I have said to you. . . .

"When the Advocate comes, whom I will send to you from the Father, the Spirit of truth who comes from the Father, he will testify on my behalf. You also are to testify because you have been with me from the beginning. . . .

"I tell you the truth: it is to your advantage that I go away, for if I do not go away, the Advocate will not come to you; but if I go, I will send him to you. And when he comes, he will prove the world wrong about sin and righteousness and judgment: about sin, because they do not believe in me; about righteousness, because I am going to the Father and you will see me no longer; about judgment, because the ruler of this world has been condemned.

"I still have many things to say to you, but you cannot bear them now. When the Spirit of truth comes, he will guide you into all truth; for he will not speak on his own, but will speak whatever he hears, and he will declare to you the things that are to come. He will glorify me, because he will take what is mine and declare it to you. All that the Father has is mine. For this reason I said that he will take what is mine and declare it to you."

Have you ever had an advocate, someone who pleaded your case before an arbitrator or a referee—or a parent or a teacher? What did he or she do for you?

Reflection Question

THINKING IT THROUGH

The above paragraphs from the Gospel of John are known by biblical scholars as the five Paraclete sayings. The word translated "advocate" that Jesus uses to describe the Holy Spirit in these verses is from the Greek word *paraclete*. It originally meant "advocate" in the legal sense—one who pleads a client's case before a court. The root of the word means "to call alongside," which denotes the helping character of the Holy Spirit.

After a brief discussion, choose someone to read this section.

When Jesus tells his disciples that he must leave them, he directs them not to worry or to be afraid, because he is going to ask the Father to send the Spirit to be their advocate, their helper. These verses describe the origin, character, and work of the Holy Spirit. Looking closely at this passage, we begin to understand the nature and effect of the Holy Spirit in the life of every Christian.

First, we see that the Holy Spirit is the Spirit of truth. He affirms what is good and pure and true and holy. However, the world—all those systems and people who base their beliefs on what can be measured and observed—cannot see the Spirit, so it doubts his existence. The invisible nature and work of the Holy Spirit makes it hard for people to believe he is real. But believers welcome the Spirit because he lives within them.

Second, the Holy Spirit functions as a teacher: he teaches believers "everything." We learn to pray with the help of the Holy Spirit. He helps us discern our spiritual gifts and then guides us in their proper use. Love, joy, peace, patience, kindness, and more come into our lives through the Holy Spirit's teaching. Like our earthly teachers, the Spirit reminds us and corrects us.

Third, the Holy Spirit functions as a witness who "testifies" about Jesus Christ. When we hear the gospel, the "good news" that Jesus Christ was born, lived, died, and rose from the dead, the Holy Spirit witnesses to our spirit that the good news is true and prompts us to accept it.

Fourth, in addition to being an advocate who defends believers, the Holy Spirit is a prosecutor who will "prove the world wrong" about its relationship to God—particularly about "sin and righteousness and judgment." We must always remember that it is the Spirit's task to convict, not ours.

Fifth, the Holy Spirit does not speak on his own but only "whatever he hears" from the Father. He speaks of what is to come, gives honor to the Son, and passes on the things of Christ and God to the believer: "He will take what is mine and declare it to you. All that the Father has is mine."

These passages provide a clear picture of the role and work of the Holy Spirit in our lives. The departure of Christ meant sorrow for the disciples, but Jesus pointed out to them, "It is to your advantage that I go away." His departure meant that now, by the work of the Holy Spirit, all believers could have individual union with Christ. By this work each believer becomes a member of Christ's spiritual body.

What's more, the Spirit is now given to empower us in our ministry. The Spirit provides us with the ability to experience the abiding presence of God, receive all truth, hear the testimony concerning Christ, convict the world of its sin, and have authority over the fallen world. Though Christ's departure grieved his disciples, it was necessary in order for the Holy Spirit to come and begin a new stage in the work of God.

Reflection Question

How do you understand the Holy Spirit's work in your own life?

GOD AND THE CHARISMATIC TRADITION

Have one member of the group read this entire section.

The Holy Spirit has been called the forgotten person of the Trinity. Since its beginning on the day of Pentecost, the Church has believed in one God comprising three persons—"God the Father, God the Son, and God the Holy Spirit"—but the Holy Spirit, an equal in the Trinity, is often neglected. We pray to God the Father in the name and authority of Jesus, the Son, and often forget the role of the Holy Spirit in our lives.

This is tragic. From the standpoint of God (as seen through the words of Jesus), the Holy Spirit *is* God—in particular, God at work in the Christian. What God the Father and God the Son began, God the Spirit continues and completes. In Michelangelo's famous painting on the ceiling of the Sistine Chapel, God is reaching out his life-giving hand to Adam and Adam is extending his hand in response. However, their fingers never quite touch. The Holy Spirit is this missing touch of God. The distance between God and his people is bridged by the Holy Spirit so that we actually become one with God.

As believers, we are temples in whom the Holy Spirit dwells (see 1 Cor. 3:16; 6:19; 2 Cor. 6:16). We are empowered by the Spirit to share the gospel that convicts and converts, to bear the fruit of the gospel in our lives (Gal. 5:22), and to exercise special gifts that enable us to build up the Church (1 Cor. 12:1–11).

God has chosen to empower those who witness about Christ, and to convict and convince those who listen to them. He has chosen to endow men and women with specific and necessary abilities that build the body of Christ, or his Church.

Most of all, he has chosen to cultivate the gospel soil of people's lives so that they bear spiritual fruit: "love, joy, peace, patience, kindness, generosity, faithfulness, gentleness, and self-control" (Gal. 5:22). Without the fruit of the Spirit, the special gifts are like a "clanging cymbal" that makes noise but has no value (1 Cor. 13:1). God lives with his people through the Holy Spirit.

The Holy Spirit empowers believers. God, as Spirit, dwells in each of us. It is our job to surrender ourselves to the awesome work of the Holy Spirit and to engage in activities that enable the Spirit to equip and empower us.

Of the Holy Spirit's fruit (love, joy, peace, patience, kindness, generosity, faithfulness, gentleness, and self-control), which has grown and matured in your life? Which has yet to bloom and grow?

Reflection Question
Allow each person a few moments to respond to this question.

WHAT IS THE CHARISMATIC TRADITION?

Without the Holy Spirit it would be impossible to practice the Six Traditions. As we have seen above, God works in the believer through the person of the Holy Spirit. The Spirit spurs the believer to pray and meditate (the focus of the Contemplative Tradition); to seek a virtuous life (the Holiness Tradition); to exercise mercy and compassion to one another (the Social Justice Tradition); to proclaim the gospel as found in the Scriptures (the Evangelical Tradition), and to promote harmony between our faith and our work (the Incarnational Tradition). However, many of us try to become faithful disciples on our own, without the power of the Holy Spirit. The vital, exciting, electrifying work of the Holy Spirit is missing in our lives. Much of our struggle with temptation and sin, along with much of our failure to live joyful, whole lives, can be traced to our unwillingness to welcome the Holy Spirit.

As before, have a member read this entire section.

The Charismatic Tradition reminds us that the Holy Spirit is absolutely essential in the Christian life. The word "charismatic" comes from the Greek word *charism*, which means "gift." Charismatic movements have always demonstrated the active work of God in people's lives in ways that make others envious or distrustful. It is here that we should note that the Charismatic Tradition (like the other Traditions) is often characterized by excess and sham. This has led many in the Church to split away and form groups that fit their particular beliefs concerning which gifts are still exercised. This is a shame.

The truth of the matter is this: God wants to be active in our lives; to endow us with supernatural abilities; to see us live with love, joy, peace, and so on. Jesus made it clear that the Holy Spirit would be sent so that he might live within us, uniting us in his body. All of us should be able to give testimony to the work of the Holy Spirit in our lives—not just those who are "charismatic" or "pentecostal." Our present task is to find ways to open ourselves to the energizing work of the living God.

Reflection Question
Give each member a chance to respond to this question if he or she wishes.

Which of the following best describes the work of the Spirit in your life? Explain your selection.

- *The Spirit has not been a major part of my spiritual life.*
- *I am beginning to see signs of the Spirit's presence in my life.*
- *The Spirit is an integral part of my spiritual life.*

PRACTICING THE CHARISMATIC TRADITION

Again, choose a member to read these paragraphs.

The Holy Spirit is received, not grasped. Neither can we coerce or bribe the Holy Spirit. In fact, many of our efforts only impede the work of the Spirit. In this sense, practicing the disciplines of the Charismatic Tradition is different from practicing those of the other five Traditions. But there are things we can do, activities that God expects us to undertake, so that the Spirit can mold and shape our lives.

To experience the ministry of the Holy Spirit, we begin by doing two things. First, we ask for the Holy Spirit (Luke 11:13). God waits for us to pray for the Spirit before he sends the One whose presence is a gift to those who simply ask. Second, we practice the discipline of waiting (Ps. 40:1). When we pray for the Spirit, we are not praying for an answer; we are asking God to enter us, to fill us with his presence, his thoughts, his words. This requires the kind of passion that takes the form of patient waiting.

What kinds of things can we expect when the Holy Spirit begins to work in our lives? While it is true that the Lord works in mysterious ways, the Bible notes several distinct ways the Spirit will work in our hearts and minds and in the lives of other people. The Holy Spirit . . .

- Gives us a sense of our unity with Christ
- Leads us into all truth
- Helps us worship God
- Guides our decision-making
- Illuminates our Bible study
- Motivates us to action
- Gives us the right words as we share our faith with others
- Softens the minds and hearts of those with whom we share our faith

These are works of the Spirit all of us can expect to see as we open ourselves to him. As you do your chosen exercise this week, be sensitive to the inner attitudes, thoughts, and feelings you are experiencing. You most likely will see God at work in ways you have never noticed before. One final caution: do not expect dramatic results or instant change. While there are many genuine works of the Holy Spirit that are immediate and life-changing, these experiences are the exception, not the rule. The Spirit works primarily by shaping the way we think, and this takes time. For example, I may pray, "Lord, give me patience—and give it to me now!" While I may desperately want to be patient, it will take time for this fruit of the Spirit to blossom and grow in my life. The fact that I desire to have more patience shows me that the Spirit is already at work, and it is my task to begin doing things that will develop the fruit. Genuine change takes time.

EXERCISES IN THE CHARISMATIC TRADITION

1. *Yield to the work of the Spirit.*
   Spend one hour in prayer this week specifically asking for the Spirit to begin working in your life in a new and powerful way. Remember, you are seeking God. Make no demands; have no expectations. Your only task is to surrender yourself to God, to open the door so that the Spirit can come in and begin changing the way you think and live. This may lead to a time of confession.

2. *Nurture the fruit of the Spirit.*
   Galatians 5:22 lists nine virtues called the fruit of the Spirit: love, joy, peace, patience, kindness, generosity, faithfulness, gentleness, and self-control. They are listed in contrast with the "works of the flesh": fornication, impurity, licentiousness, idolatry, sorcery, enmities, strife, jealousy, anger, and so on (Gal. 5:19–21). While the fruit of the Spirit slips in unawares, Paul says we are responsible for living by the Spirit and keeping in step with the Spirit, which helps the fruit grow (Gal. 5:25).

   Set aside fifteen minutes a day to meditate on the fruit of the Spirit. Ask God to show you which virtue needs to be more evident in your life. Then ask the Holy Spirit to begin working in your mind and heart, knowing that change will come through sustained communion with God.

3. *Discover your spiritual gifts.*
   First Corinthians 12:8–10 lists nine gifts of the Spirit: wisdom, knowledge, faith, healing, miraculous powers, prophecy, discernment, speaking in tongues, and the interpretation of tongues. Some people have argued that some of these particular gifts are no longer needed in the Church, but most feel that the Church still needs them. Explore these gifts through prayer, asking God to guide you to a gift (or perhaps more than one) that may be neglected and needs to be stirred up in your life or the life of your church fellowship (1 Tim. 4:14).

Have each member read over the exercises silently, or have members read them aloud, one at a time. Spend a few moments considering them as each person chooses the exercise he or she will do before the next meeting.

Read the Scriptures that refer to spiritual gifts, beginning with Romans 12:6–8, 1 Corinthians 12–14:25, and Ephesians 4:11–13. Donald Gee's book *Concerning Spiritual Gifts* is an excellent, balanced introduction to the gifts of the Spirit. Stay open to God's desire to build up, heal, and minister to the Church in all her expressions.

4. *Read the Scriptures with the Holy Spirit.*
The Holy Spirit opens our mind when we read the Bible, making us receptive to its message. More specifically, the Spirit helps us understand what the text is saying to us personally and applies its message to our particular situation. Select a passage from the Bible to reflect on. As you read, ask the Holy Spirit to highlight a verse or word that is specifically meant for you to hear. When you have discovered what God wants you to hear, spend ten to fifteen minutes reflecting on why that verse or word impressed you and what lesson you need to learn from it.

5. *Listen to the Advocate when making decisions.*
One of the most important and basic ministries of the Holy Spirit is to provide guidance (Rom. 8:14, Gal. 5:25). Do you need to make an important decision? Seek the Spirit—your Advocate—to help you. Here's how: take your concern to God in prayer. Ask God to give you direction, insight, leading. That direction may take the form of an intuitive sense; it may be a friend's advice that you sense comes from God; or it may be a door of opportunity opening or closing. In all decisions, test the Spirit by examining the Scriptures. The Spirit of God will never lead you into a decision that is contrary to the principles and commandments found in the Bible.

ENDING AND BEGINNING

Allow each member time to share which of the above exercises he or she plans to do during the week. Encourage each other in this venture. After everyone has shared, join hands in a circle and pray the Lord's Prayer aloud and in unison.

Ask for a volunteer to lead the next meeting.

Our Father, who art in heaven,
Hallowed be thy name.
Thy kingdom come,
Thy will be done,
On earth as it is in heaven.
Give us this day our daily bread;
And forgive us our trespasses
As we forgive those who trespass against us.
And lead us not into temptation,
But deliver us from evil.
For thine is the kingdom, and the power, and the glory, forever and ever.
Amen.

SESSION FIVE

Practicing the Compassionate Life

THE SOCIAL JUSTICE TRADITION

THE FOOTPRINTS OF GOD

At our last meeting each of us agreed to try one of the exercises in the Charismatic Tradition. Let's share our experiences by answering the following question:

What did you learn about God and about yourself while doing the exercise?

After a few minutes of silent prayer, open with a time of sharing that the leader begins by reading this opening paragraph and answering the question posed.

JESUS AND THE COMPASSIONATE LIFE

Gospel Passage: Matthew 25:31–46

"When the Son of Man comes in his glory, and all the angels with him, then he will sit on the throne of his glory. All the nations will be gathered before him, and he will separate people one from another as a shepherd separates the sheep from the goats, and he will put the sheep at his right hand and the goats at the left. Then the king will say to those at his right hand, 'Come, you that are blessed by my Father, inherit the kingdom prepared for you from the foundation of the world; for I was hungry and you gave me food, I was thirsty and you gave me something to drink, I was a stranger and you welcomed me, I was naked and you gave me clothing, I was sick and you took care of me, I was in prison and you visited me.' Then the righteous will answer him, 'Lord, when was it that we saw you hungry and gave you food, or thirsty and gave you something to drink? And when was it that we saw you a stranger and welcomed you, or naked and gave you clothing? And when was it that we saw you sick or in prison and visited you?' And the

When everyone has had a chance to respond, ask a member to read this Scripture passage.

51

king will answer them, 'Truly I tell you, just as you did it to one of the least of these who are members of my family, you did it to me.' Then he will say to those at his left hand, 'You that are accursed, depart from me into the eternal fire prepared for the devil and his angels; for I was hungry and you gave me no food, I was thirsty and you gave me nothing to drink, I was a stranger and you did not welcome me, naked and you did not give me clothing, sick and in prison and you did not visit me.' Then they also will answer, 'Lord, when was it that we saw you hungry or thirsty or a stranger or naked or sick or in prison, and did not take care of you?' Then he will answer them, 'Truly I tell you, just as you did not do it to one of the least of these, you did not do it to me.' And these will go away into eternal punishment, but the righteous into eternal life."

Reflection Question

Have you ever been a stranger? Describe some of the feelings you had. Did anyone welcome you? Describe that experience.

THINKING IT THROUGH

After a brief discussion, choose someone to read this section.

This passage from the Gospel of Matthew is a powerful indictment of those who neglect the needy. Though it reads like a parable, it actually describes the future judgment of all the nations. Jesus uses a simile ("He will separate people one from another *as* a shepherd separates the sheep from the goats") to give us a mental picture of what that reckoning will be like. Jesus, like a shepherd, will separate all people into two groups: those who cared for the needs of the hungry, thirsty, alienated, naked, sick, or jailed; and those who did not.

One detail about the judgment towers above all others: Jesus tells his listeners that when they have (or have not) cared for the needy, they have (or have not) cared for *him*. When Jesus blesses the first group, they are surprised and ask, "When did we see you . . . ?" They remember helping the needy, but they do not recall serving food to Jesus in a soup kitchen, or giving water to Jesus in the desert, or welcoming Jesus into their fellowship, or buying clothes for Jesus during a recession, or caring for Jesus in a nursing home, or visiting Jesus in a penitentiary. Though the second group never did these things, they offer the same plea: "Lord, when was it that we saw you . . . ?" Jesus then delivers his powerful punch line: he says, in effect, "Truly I tell you, just as you helped [or did not help] the people who needed it the most, you helped [or did not help] me." Jesus' reply stresses that when we serve the needy, we actually serve him.

The picture of the judgment becomes all the more vivid when we note that both groups call Jesus "Lord." But in Matthew 7:21 Jesus says, "Not everyone who says to me, 'Lord, Lord,' will enter the kingdom of heaven, but only the one who does the will of my Father in heaven." The judgment standard is not that they recognize Jesus as Lord, but rather that they do the will of God by meeting the physical and spiritual needs of Jesus' family.

We may be tempted to turn this teaching into a law that we must follow or a dogma that says we can become friends with God by doing good deeds ("works righteousness"). Here we must be careful. Martin Luther said that "Christ did not free us from the law; he freed us from a wrong understanding of the law." The "wrong understanding" that Luther refers to is the belief that we can restore our relationship with God by observing the law, or by doing good works. Christ frees us from these soul-killing notions. But the fact that we have been saved by grace through faith—"this is not your own doing; it is the gift of God"—does not free us from our responsibility to do God's will (Eph. 2:8). In fact, our faith increases, not decreases, our responsibility. We are not free to neglect the needy. We cannot hide under our "faith umbrella" and neglect those who need our help. Jesus told his disciples about the final judgment, and the account has been passed on to warn us that he expects more, not less, from those who call him "Lord."

Besides the six groups of needy people mentioned in Matthew 25, who else fits into the "least of these" category?

Reflection Question

GOD AND THE SOCIAL JUSTICE TRADITION

God cares deeply about how we treat one another. When asked which commandment in the law is greatest, Jesus responded, "'You shall love the Lord your God with all your heart, and with all your soul, and with all your mind.' This is the greatest and first commandment. And a second is like it: 'You shall love your neighbor as yourself.' On these two commandments hang all the law and the prophets" (Matt. 22:37–40). As we discussed in Session 3, the commandments are God's instructions to us: he gave them to us so that we know how to act. The call to love one another is grounded in God's love for us. God loves us, so we should also love one another (1 John 4:11). Jesus too said, "Just as I have loved you, you also should love one another" (John 13:34). God reveals his love for us through the commandments and the birth, life, death, and resurrection of Jesus Christ, and he expects us to respond by loving him and one another.

Have one member of the group read this entire section.

When we look at the call to practice social justice from God's perspective, we see it much differently. Each and every human being—in fact, the entire universe—is a precious work of God. The book of Proverbs tells us, "Those who oppress the poor insult their Maker, but those who are kind to the needy honor him" (Prov. 14:31). If we could see the world through the eyes of God, we would look through a filter of compassion. God cares about our needs, our hurts, our brokenness. He understands our sinfulness—it does not shock or surprise him. And instead of judging us, God is ready to forgive, to heal, to restore us. We are all precious in God's sight, and the Lord longs for us to see others as he does—priceless, unique people who need love and compassion.

Jesus lived a life of compassion for "the least." He mended and cared for the sick, he forgave the sinful, and he shared meals with prostitutes and tax collectors. Yet his compassion never undermined his sense of justice. Rather, he blended the two together. His love of God led him to grab a whip and throw out the merchants in the temple. When faced with injustice, Jesus fought against it with a holy passion. In Isaiah God states that "I the LORD love justice" (61:8). Numerous Old Testament prophets proclaimed the justice of God by addressing certain nations and their treatment of the poor and oppressed. The Psalmist declared, "The LORD works vindication and justice for all who are oppressed" (Ps. 103:6).

God desires that we "give justice to the weak and the orphan; maintain the right of the lowly and the destitute" (Ps. 82:3). In the words of the prophet Micah and others, he *tells* us how to live:

He has told you, O mortal, what is good;
   and what does the LORD require of you
but to do justice, and to love kindness,
   and to walk humbly with your God? (Micah 6:8)

And in the person of Jesus Christ God *shows* us how to live.

Reflection Question
Allow each person a few moments to respond to these questions.

Have you ever been unjustly treated? Have you seen another person being oppressed? How did you respond?

WHAT IS THE SOCIAL JUSTICE TRADITION?

As before, have a member read this entire section.

As we saw in the last section, Jesus distilled the law into two commandments: love God and love your neighbor. According to Luke's Gospel, a fellow Jew then asked Jesus, "And who is my neighbor?" Jesus answered the question by telling him a parable about a person whom the Jews considered unclean—a Samaritan—who stopped to help a man who had been robbed, stripped, beaten, and left beside the road to die. A Jewish priest and a Levite had seen the needy man but had passed by him without bothering to stop and help. The Samaritan, when he came along, treated and bandaged the man's wounds, boosted him onto his own animal, took him to an inn, cared for him for a day, and then paid the innkeeper for his extended care. After telling the parable, Jesus asked the questioner, "Which of these three, do you think, was a neighbor to the man?" and he responded, "'The one who showed him mercy.' Jesus said to him, 'Go and do likewise'" (10:29–37).

The Social Justice Tradition has always been integral to the life of the Church, emphasizing our responsibility and mandate to love our neighbor. Throughout the history of the Church men and women have dedicated their lives to caring for the hungry, the poor, the naked, the alienated, the sick, and the imprisoned. Their influence upon the Church has been dramatic. For example, the Salvation Army has extended a helping hand to our poor and needy inner-city neighbors for over a century. Mother Teresa's Sisters of Mercy pick up destitute people from the streets of Calcutta, nurse the sick back to health, and help the dying leave this world with dignity. World Vision and other relief efforts send food and medical care to people who would starve to death or die of disease without help. These touching, genuine, compassionate responses to human need—and others too numerous to mention—testify to God's tender love.

Often the compassionate response demands more than a shipment of food or medicine, however. There is an old proverb that says, "Give a man a fish, and you have fed him for one day; teach him to fish, and you have fed him for a lifetime." Many times bringing justice into a situation goes beyond temporary assistance; it involves helping people learn skills so that they can support themselves. The poor and the homeless need not only immediate food and shelter, but also ongoing help to overcome their plight. Many societal structures and institutions actually oppress needy people by denying them access to certain occupations, job promotions, essential services, educational opportunities, adequate housing, and more. Christ calls us to fight policies that discriminate on the basis of external appearances such as race and gender and social backgrounds such as class and religion, and to stand against societies and governments that oppress their people by denying them basic human rights. The Social Justice Tradition has always called the Church to work for equity in all human relations and social structures. So must we if we truly love our neighbor.

What are some factors that keep us from getting involved in social justice activities?

Reflection Question
Give each member a chance to respond to this question if he or she wishes.

PRACTICING THE SOCIAL JUSTICE TRADITION

One of the most remarkable aspects of practicing the Social Justice Tradition is its double effect: in the process of helping others, we too are helped. John Wesley once said that true happiness comes from helping others. We begin the task of "carrying one another's burdens" out of compassion, but in the end we find that we too have been truly blessed.

There is, however, a pitfall we should be aware of before we enter into any project of service as part of practicing the Social Justice Tradition. In his book *Celebration of Discipline* Richard Foster notes the important difference between self-righteous service and true service (pp. 128–130). He lists nine points to consider as we engage in works of compassion:

Again, choose a member to read these paragraphs.

- Self-righteous service relies on human effort, whereas true service flows out of a relationship with God. Listen to the promptings of God as you begin and lean on his strength to do the task.

Have different members of the group take turns reading the following list.

- Self-righteous service is impressed with the "big deal," whereas true service makes no distinction between the large and the small. Be indiscriminate in your choice, knowing that God often considers the small task the most important.

- Self-righteous service requires external rewards, whereas true service rests contented in hiddenness. Avoid doing things for others as a means of getting applause or reward, relying instead on the divine nod of approval.

- Self-righteous service is concerned with results, whereas true service is free of the need to calculate them. Do not let your expectations guide your service, and do not be disappointed if your service effects no external change.

- Self-righteous service picks and chooses whom to serve, whereas true service is indiscriminate in its ministry. Be careful not to neglect the poor and the lowly in favor of the rich and powerful—or vice versa!

- Self-righteous service is affected by moods and whims, whereas true service ministers on the basis of need. Do not let your feelings, which ebb and flow, determine your actions; rather, let the service discipline your feelings.

- Self-righteous service is temporary, whereas true service is ongoing. Compassion is a way of life that spontaneously meets human need, not merely an occasional helping hand.

- Self-righteous service is insensitive, whereas true service withholds as freely as it gives. Listen with tenderness and patience before you begin. Be sensitive to what people really need, not merely what *you* think they need.

- Self-righteous service fractures community, whereas true service builds community. Be careful not to let your "good works" become debts that others must repay. Direct your efforts toward building unity in the community.

These guidelines will be extremely important as you do one of the following acts of service. The best way to start your task this week is to begin with this simple prayer: "Lord Jesus, show me someone whom I can serve." God loves to answer this prayer.

EXERCISES IN THE SOCIAL JUSTICE TRADITION

1. *Write a kind, encouraging letter.*

   This may seem like a small task, but it can work miracles. Take time to write a letter that tells someone how important he or she is to you. We seldom let people know how much they are appreciated. Or perhaps you know someone who is struggling with something—a decision, a failed marriage, a disappointment. Write a letter that tells him or her that you care and that you are available to talk or listen. "Anxiety weighs down the human heart, but a good word cheers it up" (Prov. 12:25).

2. *Volunteer to help at a local food bank or soup kitchen.*

   Relief efforts and service organizations always need helping hands. Look in the telephone book or ask someone in your church for the name of a food bank or soup kitchen. Call and volunteer to help in any area. Such organizations usually need workers to stock shelves, serve food, clean storerooms, do clerical work, and undertake other such tasks. A few hours of your time will be greatly appreciated.

3. *Guard the reputation of another person.*

   Although you cannot see it, a person's reputation is valuable, and you can guard and protect it by refusing to gossip or backbite. Paul urged Titus "to speak evil of no one" (3:2a). By refusing to take part in discussions that focus on half-truths or fault-finding, you can contribute to the death of a rumor or criticism. If people you are talking with start to say things that are gossipy or critical of someone, smile and gently say, "We don't know that's really true, do we?" or "That doesn't sound like him [or her] at all." Then simply change the subject. Your gentle demeanor and response in protecting another person's valuable reputation can help others become aware of the harmful nature of their words.

4. *Look for an injustice and address it.*

   If you open your eyes, you will begin to see areas in your home, workplace, community, and church that support injustice. As a first step, examine yourself to make sure that you are not looking for a speck in your neighbor's eye and overlooking the two-by-four in your own (Matt. 7:3–5). In other words, ask yourself, "Am I doing something that oppresses someone else?" Look for ways you might be taking advantage of someone, abusing that person's kindness, or stifling his or her growth. After a thorough self-examination you will be more able to look at the injustice around you.

   You should always avoid advising people on a problem or condemning them for their actions, but if you are true to the task of addressing injustice, you will—at some point—need to voice your concern. For example, if someone in your workplace is doing something unethical (perhaps lying to customers about a product), you can bring

Have each member read over the exercises silently, or have members read them aloud, one at a time. Spend a few moments considering them as each person chooses the exercise he or she will do before the next meeting.

the issue up with your coworker in a calm, tactful, and non-accusatory manner. Remember, the goal is not to hurt people but to see justice reign.

5. *Take a stand.*

    Is there racism, sexism, or some other form of discrimination in a club or a business or a community or an institution that you need to address? If so, discuss with the Spiritual Formation Group what your response should be. If your action involves some form of civil disobedience, engage in it peacefully, prayerfully, and compassionately. Be sure that the other members of the group support you with prayer and other appropriate actions.

ENDING AND BEGINNING

Allow each member time to share which of the above exercises he or she plans to do during the week. Encourage each other in this venture. After everyone has shared, join hands in a circle and pray the Lord's Prayer aloud and in unison.

Ask for a volunteer to lead the next meeting.

Our Father, who art in heaven,
Hallowed be thy name.
Thy kingdom come,
Thy will be done,
On earth as it is in heaven.
Give us this day our daily bread;
And forgive us our trespasses
As we forgive those who trespass against us.
And lead us not into temptation,
But deliver us from evil.
For thine is the kingdom, and the power, and the glory, forever and ever.
Amen.

SESSION SIX

Practicing the Word-Centered Life

THE EVANGELICAL TRADITION

THE FOOTPRINTS OF GOD

At our last meeting each of us agreed to try one of the exercises in the Social Justice Tradition. Let's share our experiences by answering the following question:

What did you learn about God and about yourself while doing the exercise?

After a few minutes of silent prayer, open with a time of sharing that the leader begins by reading this opening paragraph and answering the question posed.

JESUS AND THE WORD-CENTERED LIFE

Gospel Passage: Luke 4:16–20a; 42–44

When he came to Nazareth, where he had been brought up, he went to the synagogue on the sabbath day, as was his custom. He stood up to read, and the scroll of the prophet Isaiah was given to him. He unrolled the scroll and found the place where it was written:

When everyone has had a chance to respond, ask a member to read this Scripture passage.

> "The Spirit of the Lord is upon me,
>   because he has anointed me to bring good news to the poor.
> He has sent me to proclaim release to the captives
>   and recovery of sight to the blind,
>   to let the oppressed go free,
> to proclaim the year of the Lord's favor."

And he rolled up the scroll, gave it back to the attendant, and sat down. . . .

At daybreak he departed and went into a deserted place. And the crowds were looking for him; and when they reached him, they wanted to prevent him from leaving them. But he said to them, "I must proclaim the good news of the kingdom of God to the other cities also; for I was sent for this purpose." So he continued proclaiming the message in the synagogues of Judea.

Reflection Question

How did you first become aware of the good news of the kingdom of God? Did you hear it proclaimed by a person, or did you read about it in the Bible?

THINKING IT THROUGH

After a brief discussion, choose someone to read this section.

In these two passages from Luke's Gospel we see Jesus at the beginning of his ministry. He has traveled from Judea, where he was baptized by John in the Jordan River, fasted for forty days and nights in the nearby desert, and overcame the devil's three temptations. Filled with the power of the Spirit, he goes to his home region, Galilee, and teaches in its synagogues, receiving praise from everyone.

But being praised by Galileans was not always a compliment. Residents of Galilee were considered backward by their fellow Jews, the Judeans, for several reasons: Galilee was physically cut off from Judea by Samaria, much of its population lived in small towns, and its economy centered around agriculture and cottage industries. Today we might say that Judeans considered Galileans "crude and rude" while they viewed themselves as "refined and cultured." In fact, Galilee had been isolated from mainstream Jewish life for so long that its residents had a distinct accent (Matt. 26:73).

But it is among the plain, ordinary, scorned folk of Galilee that Jesus begins his ministry. Early in his travels, he comes to Nazareth and worships in the synagogue on the Sabbath. And it is to his former neighbors that he, the living Word of God, explicitly proclaims the good news of the kingdom of God from the Scriptures, the written word of God, and points to himself as the fulfillment of the passage from Isaiah.

We must understand the shock that Jesus' hearers feel before we can fully appreciate Jesus' action. For centuries these Galileans have hoped and waited for a deliverer, a Messiah who will free them from political oppression. Every Sabbath they go to their local synagogue to sing psalms, pray for the Messiah to come, and listen to the Scriptures, depending upon their rabbi to interpret the sacred texts. They have waited and waited. Numerous self-proclaimed Messiahs have lived . . . and died. Between Sabbaths many times their hope has died when they have been confronted by cruel soldiers or greedy tax collectors, but each time it has come alive again when they listen to the promises of Scripture.

Now here is the village carpenter—this man they know as the son of Joseph and Mary, this man who grew up in Nazareth—claiming to be the anointed one, the Messiah, and proclaiming "the year of the Lord's favor." *Who does he think he is? Any fool knows that the Messiah is to come from Bethlehem! What is this kingdom of God stuff? We want our own country! And what does he think he's doing, explaining Scripture in that way?* They become enraged and try, but fail, to throw Jesus over a cliff. However, their reaction does not stop him. He continues to focus on the *euangelion*, the proclamation of "the good news of the kingdom of God" throughout Galilee and in the synagogues of Judea—and even in Jerusalem, the center of Judaism.

How does Jesus speak the good news of "release to the captives" to your life?

Reflection Question

GOD AND THE EVANGELICAL TRADITION

God uses three central ways to reveal himself to us: the written word, the living Word, and the spoken word. Most of us are familiar with the Bible, the word of God written. The first section, the Hebrew law (or Torah), includes the Ten Commandments and was written first on tablets, then on rolled scrolls of parchment that were passed from generation to generation. Later the Hebrews added the scriptural components known as the "Prophets" and the "Writings." God has used the Scriptures to communicate directly with his people for millennia. Like the early Hebrews, their descendants believe that the Scriptures are sacred and handle them with great care. They view them as God's actual words that were transcribed by ordinary human beings. Tradition tells us that when a Jewish scribe copies the books of the Scriptures, he washes his hands before he writes the word "God."

Have one member of the group read this entire section.

Christians call the Hebrew Scriptures the "Old Testament" and add other writings called the "New Testament" to form the Bible. (Some Christians add a third section called the "Apocrypha," which tells the history of the Israelites between the Old and New Testaments.) In the New Testament we learn about Jesus in the Gospels, the beginnings of the Church in Acts, faithful living in the Epistles, and our ultimate destiny in Revelation. Christians know the two testaments together as the written word of God and hold both in high esteem because from them we learn about God.

The living Word, Jesus Christ, is God's clearest expression of himself and statement of his purposes. John 1:1 states, "In the beginning was the Word [the Logos], and the Word was with God, and the Word was God." As the Logos, Jesus reveals to us a God who creates, who loves, who heals, who understands, who blesses. God became one of us to show himself to us and to bring us back into his family. When we look into the face of Jesus, we see God. We see eyes that radiate compassion and lips that say "God loves you." We see God, because Jesus *is* God.

It is impossible to express fully the mystery of Jesus as the living Word. In Colossians, Paul tells us that Christ "is the image of the invisible God, the firstborn of all creation; for in him all things in heaven and on earth were cre-ated, things visible and invisible. . . . He himself is before all things, and in him all things hold together" (1:15–16a; 17). We owe our very being and our day-to-day welfare to Jesus Christ, the living Word. Thanksgiving can be our only response.

But it is the spoken word of God, the proclamation of the gospel, that is at the core of the Word-centered life. The role of a word is to communicate. It conveys an idea or a meaning. We use words in order to have a relation-ship with another person; through words we connect with each other. In talking about our faith, we speak the written word (the Bible) that tells about the living Word (Jesus Christ) so that hearers can establish a relationship with God.

With spoken words we proclaim the gospel to those who have not heard: "So faith comes from what is heard, and what is heard comes through the word of Christ" (Rom. 10:17). We are witnesses to the person of Jesus Christ, whose story resides in the Bible, and we use words to tell the good news to everyone—those who can read and those who cannot. Our task is to proclaim not our own words but God's Word to the nations.

Reflection Question
Allow each person a few moments to respond to this question.

How has the proclamation of the gospel of Jesus Christ influenced your life? Describe its effects.

WHAT IS THE EVANGELICAL TRADITION?

As before, have a member read this entire section.

As we saw above, the Evangelical Tradition emphasizes the proclamation—the *euangelion*—of the gospel of Jesus Christ. In Romans, Paul asserts, "Everyone who calls on the name of the Lord shall be saved"; but then he asks, "But how are they to call on one in whom they have not believed? And how are they to believe in one of whom they have never heard? And how are they to hear without someone to proclaim him? And how are they to pro-claim him unless they are sent? As it is written, 'How beautiful are the feet of those who bring good news!'" (10:13–15).

By working backward, we can see the flow of the Evangelical Tradition and its practice: First, a person must be sent to those who have not heard the word of God. Second, the messenger must proclaim the word, or witness to it. Third, the listener must receive the word and believe. Fourth, the listener must ask God to restore their relationship. Again the words of Paul: "Faith comes from what is heard, and what is heard comes through the word of Christ" (Rom. 10:17).

And what is this "good news of the kingdom of God"? God the Son entered history, bringing with him the message that the Father longs for us to return home, to respond to his love, to come close to his heart. And Jesus tells us that he is the way back into God's love, back into God's care, back into God's life. He reveals the kingdom of God to us—a kingdom that is full of joy and love and peace. When we look at Jesus, we see not only God, but the kingdom too.

When the Pharisees asked Jesus when the kingdom would come, he responded, "The kingdom of God is not coming with signs to be observed; nor will they say, 'Look, here it is!' Or 'There it is!' For behold, the kingdom of God is in your midst" (Luke 17:20b–21, NASB). And the kingdom in our midst—the life of God—is available to everyone who hears the *euangelion* of the gospel. This is the heart of the Evangelical Tradition.

Many of us learned that evangelism alone was at the heart of the Evangelical Tradition. Does the concept that the Evangelical Tradition includes the written word, the living Word, and the proclamation of the gospel help or hinder you? Explain.

Reflection Question
Give each member a chance to respond to this question if he or she wishes.

PRACTICING THE EVANGELICAL TRADITION

When we talk about the three main aspects of the Evangelical Tradition— the Bible, Jesus Christ, and proclamation—many of us feel anxious. For a lot of people, the Bible is a very difficult book to read, much less understand. Others may not be ready to believe that Jesus Christ is the living Word, the Son of God; they may feel that they need to have more faith. Many of us are often hesitant about proclaiming the gospel, fearing that we will offend someone or sound "preachy."

Again, choose a member to read these paragraphs.

These are legitimate fears. The Bible is *not* always easily read or understood. Many times belief in Jesus Christ's full identity *does* come only gradually, as we grow spiritually. And it *is* easy for our words to be rejected when we discuss the gospel of Jesus Christ with someone. But these fears should not prevent us from taking small steps so that our ability and faith gradually increase and we can take big steps. The following suggestions may help ease our fears.

A contemporary translation of the Bible is much easier to read than an older one such as the King James Version. While the King James language is beautiful, the centuries-old wording can be difficult to understand. A translation such as the New Revised Standard Version (used in these lessons) or a paraphrase-translation such as *The Message* can help people get into the practice of using the Bible regularly.

Keep in mind that we are reading the Bible with an ear to what God is saying to us, not simply studying it like a textbook. On one level we are trying to understand its message—what is it saying? what is the main point?— but at a deeper level we are interacting with words that will mold and shape our thoughts and our hearts. For this spiritual formation to take place, we should read the Bible slowly, repeating each verse several times, letting the words sink deep into our spirit.

We ask Jesus Christ to increase our faith in him. James says that "you do not have, because you do not ask" (4:2b). Then, with the certainty that God will grant our request, we act. We read the four Gospels—Matthew, Mark, Luke, and John, books that contain a record of Jesus' birth, life, death, and resurrection—over and over. We see Jesus as a newborn baby. We watch him heal the sick and exorcise the possessed. We observe him confounding the "religious" experts. We walk with him down the dusty roads of Galilee, Judea, and Samaria. We listen to his teachings. We weep with him at the tomb of Lazarus. And more. We get Jesus into us. And while we are getting Jesus into us, we claim the verse "Faith is the assurance of things hoped for, the conviction of things not seen," trusting that God will increase our belief (Heb. 11:1).

When sharing the gospel, we need to remember that we are simply to tell others what God has done; it is not our job to convert anyone. If we emphasize changing those we share the gospel with, we will end up frustrated, and they, sensing our true motives, will be offended that we think they need to change. By keeping the focus on what God has done to bring humankind back into relationship with him, and on the love and joy and peace that Jesus Christ is bringing into our lives, we will make them hungry for what we have. They will want to know more about the God we are talking about. We should always keep in mind that the Holy Spirit draws, not coerces, people into the kingdom of God.

EXERCISES IN THE EVANGELICAL TRADITION

Have each member read over the exercises silently, or have members read them aloud, one at a time. Spend a few moments considering them as each person chooses the exercise he or she will do before the next meeting.

1. *Memorize a verse of Scripture.*
   Select a verse unfamiliar to you from a favorite translation. You may want to pick one of these excellent verses—Galatians 2:20, Romans 5:1, John 3:16, Psalm 1:1, Ephesians 2:8—or you may want to choose some other verse. Memorizing Scripture allows God's word to take root in your thought-life and in your inner heart. It is easier to memorize a verse one phrase at a time than all at once. Keep adding phrases and saying the verse to yourself throughout the day until you are able to repeat it from memory.

2. *Read one of the shorter books of the Bible out loud.*
   The Gospels, and even Paul's letters, were read aloud to the early Christians in their gathered communities. Read one of Paul's shorter letters (for example, Galatians, Ephesians, Philippians, Colossians, 1 and 2 Timothy, 1 and 2 Thessalonians, Titus) out loud to yourself. Imagine how the Christians listening to those words for the first time felt and responded.

3. *Meditate on a verse or brief passage about Jesus Christ.*
    Keep your selection simple: for example, John 1:1, John 1:14, Hebrews
    1:1–2, or 1 John 1:1–3. Take twenty minutes or so to read the verse or
    passage slowly and carefully. Pause after each sentence and reflect on it.
    Ask questions: What does this sentence mean? What is God telling me
    about himself? about Jesus Christ? about me? about others? If a partic-
    ular word or phrase stands out, spend additional time reflecting on it.

4. *Imagine yourself as one of Jesus' brothers.*
    Read John 7:1–8. You have known Jesus since you were born; he is your
    older brother. You grew up in the same house and worked together in
    the carpentry shop. But he is acting crazy, going around the countryside
    healing people and preaching to crowds and making outlandish claims.
    Yet Jesus wants to keep out of the public eye. How do his actions make
    you feel? Do you feel ashamed? proud? angry? jealous? willing to side
    with his enemies? Do you share some of the same doubt Jesus' brothers
    did? If so, ask Jesus to help you overcome it.

5. *Look for an opportunity to tell someone about your faith.*
    Prayer precedes these opportunities, so begin by praying that God will
    bring you into contact with someone who needs to hear about Jesus.
    Ask God to let you know in some way who is the right person and
    when is the right time. When that person asks how you are doing, or
    how things are going, gently begin speaking about the central place
    faith in Jesus Christ has in your life. Do not speak in a way that makes
    the person feel he or she is being judged or manipulated. Simply
    express what has happened to you and let that word go forth simply
    and honestly.

6. *Proclaim the gospel by your actions.*
    St. Francis reminds us, "Always preach Christ; use words when neces-
    sary." During the next few days let your actions speak for you, but
    before beginning, pray for the insight to see your life as others see it.
    Then as you come into contact with people, pay particular attention to
    your actions and what they are conveying. The fruit of the Spirit (love,
    joy, peace, and so on) witnesses to the power of God. When people see
    these qualities in your life, they will instinctively want to know what
    makes you "different." By the end of this exercise you should be able to
    pick out areas in your life that speak well of Christ and areas that need
    correcting.

ENDING AND BEGINNING

Allow each member time to share which of the above exercises he or she plans to do during the week. Encourage each other in this venture. After everyone has shared, join hands in a circle and pray the Lord's Prayer aloud and in unison.

Ask for a volunteer to lead the next meeting.

Our Father, who art in heaven,
Hallowed be thy name.
Thy kingdom come,
Thy will be done,
On earth as it is in heaven.
Give us this day our daily bread;
And forgive us our trespasses
As we forgive those who trespass against us.
And lead us not into temptation,
But deliver us from evil.
For thine is the kingdom, and the power, and the glory, forever and ever.
Amen.

Practicing the Sacramental Life

THE INCARNATIONAL TRADITION

THE FOOTPRINTS OF GOD

At our last meeting each of us agreed to try one of the exercises in the Evangelical Tradition. Let's share our experiences by answering the following question:

What did you learn about God and about yourself while doing the exercise?

After a few minutes of silent prayer, open with a time of sharing that the leader begins by reading this opening paragraph and answering the question posed.

JESUS AND THE SACRAMENTAL LIFE

Gospel Passage: Luke 13:10–17

Now he was teaching in one of the synagogues on the sabbath. And just then there appeared a woman with a spirit that had crippled her for eighteen years. She was bent over and was quite unable to stand up straight. When Jesus saw her, he called her over and said, "Woman, you are set free from your ailment." When he laid his hands on her, immediately she stood up straight and began praising God. But the leader of the synagogue, indignant because Jesus had cured on the sabbath, kept saying to the crowd, "There are six days on which work ought to be done; come on those days and be cured, and not on the sabbath day." But the Lord answered him and said, "You hypocrites! Does not each of you on the sabbath untie his ox or his donkey from the manger, and lead it away to give it water? And ought not this woman, a daughter of Abraham whom Satan bound for eighteen long years, be set free from this bondage on the sabbath day?" When he said this, all his opponents were put to shame; and the entire crowd was rejoicing at all the wonderful things that he was doing.

When everyone has had a chance to respond, ask a member to read this Scripture passage.

Reflection Question

Do you ever feel guilty for doing work on what many consider a "holy" day, such as Sunday or Easter or Christmas? If you do, why?

THINKING IT THROUGH

After a brief discussion, choose someone to read this section.

In this passage from Luke's Gospel we confront the age-old division between work and faith. People, especially religious leaders, have tried to erect a wall between the two for millennia. In our time the business world is helping to fortify that wall, as is American culture in general: we see the work-faith issue in church/state debates over the place of religion in schools, legislative bodies, the courts, and more. Can children read a Bible during study break? Can a governing body open its meetings with prayer? Can judges post the Ten Commandments in their courtrooms? And on and on.

Jesus faced this dichotomy head on. Before we consider his response, though, we need to look at some background. Jesus had been teaching in synagogues on the Sabbath since the early part of his ministry. This was nothing new. He had become known throughout Galilee and Judea for his succinct, powerful lessons.

First-century synagogue services were similar to our present-day church services. The people sang songs (psalms), listened to the reading of Scripture, prayed, and heard a message, normally delivered by the local rabbi. But in this service Jesus was what we might call the "guest speaker." We do not know whether the leader invited him to speak or whether he was the guest of someone who belonged to the synagogue. In either case, he was bringing the "message" on the Sabbath and worshiping with the local people.

But right in the middle of his talk "there appeared a woman," an unusual happening in itself. Most archaeologists believe that men worshiped on the ground floor of synagogues while women observed the service from the balcony. If this is true, then any woman who "appeared" among the men was not where she was supposed to be. The description of this woman's infirmity suggests that she may have been unable to go up the stairs to the balcony. In that case, she may have come late to the service and tried to slip in unnoticed.

Jesus did what he was called to do—"let the oppressed go free" (see Session 6)—and healed the woman. The leader then became furious and tried to regain control of his synagogue. He reminded worshipers that religious law was very clear about when work should be done—during the week, never on the Sabbath. And healing on the Sabbath was "work." So Jesus responded with an illustration everyone readily understood: *You two-faced legalists will work on the Sabbath to take your animals to water and keep them alive*—he said, in effect—*but you won't lift a finger to help this woman! Are they worth more than she is?*

We see no division between sacred and secular in the words and deeds of Jesus. In this Gospel passage, who Jesus was at the core of his being flowed out in an act of mercy as he observed the sacraments of his Jewish faith, shattering the fragile wall separating faith and work, sacred and secular.

How do you think you would respond if your minister stopped speaking to heal a woman? Or if a homeless person walked down the aisle during the middle of a choir number and asked the minister for money to rent an apartment?

Reflection Question

GOD AND THE INCARNATIONAL TRADITION

We briefly mentioned the Trinity—Father, Son, and Holy Spirit—in Session 4, when we discussed the Charismatic Tradition. Here we must treat it in greater depth because of the nature of the Incarnational Tradition.

Have one member of the group read this entire section.

The doctrine of the Trinity is one of the most controversial and most profound teachings of the Church. Countless people have abandoned the Church, canceling their membership or starting their own fellowship, because they could not accept one or another of the Trinity as God. Numberless volumes trying to explain the relationship between Father, Son, and Holy Spirit have been written. Even other religions get involved in the debate, accusing Christians of worshiping three Gods. Clearly, then, the teaching is not easily understood or communicated.

But the Trinity is at the heart of the Incarnational Tradition, because Jesus Christ *is* the Incarnation. In the person of Jesus Christ, God became human, thereby putting his blessing upon the material, physical world in which we live. God as Spirit created a physical body to inhabit—a marvelous, wondrous, indescribable reality harmonizing spirit and matter. By taking on all of the limitations of physical existence and living among us, God told us without words that he loves matter; and because we are made of matter, what we say, what we do, and who we are is invaluable. God created humans as embodied spirits, and when he saw that we had lost our way, he became one of us—Jesus—to help us find our way back into his family.

As part of his earthly life, Jesus regularly attended local synagogues, worshiping and taking part in the practices of his faith. The Gospels also record that he went to Jerusalem often to pray and worship at the temple. Though we may disdain or recoil from one "sacrament" of early Judaism— animal sacrifice—we have no record that Jesus shunned its practice. In fact, Luke's Gospel tells us that Jesus' parents offered (killed) two birds when they presented him in the temple (2:22–24). Just as God affirmed matter by becoming human, so he affirms our sacraments and our liturgies, which are rooted in the physical.

Contrary to what some people think, though, God does not confine his affirmation of human activity to those actions we consider "religious," important as they are. By growing up in a family and taking part in everyday human activities such as working, eating, laughing, washing, walking, weeping, talking, and more, Jesus put his imprimatur, his "stamp of approval," on every aspect of human life. Nothing was exempt; everything received equal honor.

Likewise, Jesus affirmed our vocations, both blue-collar and white-collar, by becoming an ordinary laborer—a carpenter—and a teacher—a rabbi. Most paintings and films portray Jesus as a slight, pale-skinned man with soft, uncallused hands. But we ought to imagine him as robust and dark-skinned with rough, scarred hands capable of transforming raw wood into a cradle as smooth and unblemished as a baby's skin. His transformative powers were equally effective in speaking: when Jesus taught, "people were spellbound by what they heard" (Luke 19:48), which tells us that his words were full of wisdom and power.

In the Incarnation, God affirmed the value of human life and the goodness of the entire material world.

Reflection Question
Allow each person a few moments to respond to this question.

Have you ever considered that the everyday aspects of your life—cleaning house, loving your spouse, going to work—are as important to God as the spiritual aspects? Discuss.

WHAT IS THE INCARNATIONAL TRADITION?

As before, have a member read this entire section.

We have discussed God the Father's affirmation of all life in becoming a human—God the Son—but we have not addressed the role of God the Holy Spirit in the Incarnational Tradition. As we learned in Session 4, the Holy Spirit dwells in the children of God, and his presence is necessary for us to practice the Traditions. This is particularly true of the Incarnational Tradition.

As physical beings we find it easy to focus on the material—the things we can see and touch. We need food to live and we enjoy eating. Our bodies get cold so we buy clothes. When we hit our thumb with a hammer, it hurts until we take a painkiller. Because we are sentient beings, everything we know about ourselves, other people, and our world comes through our senses. We are matter ourselves, so we perceive matter easily.

This presents a huge problem when we start exploring the world of the spirit. We cannot smell, taste, touch, see, or hear the spiritual, so we hesitate to believe it is real. We relegate it to a special category, a "pigeonhole," allowing it out only on special "holy" days or when we have a specific need (such as a need for physical healing).

The Holy Spirit helps us overcome this disunity by promoting the harmony of the physical and the spiritual. At their creation, Adam and Eve's bodies and spirits were in perfect harmony. But at the fall, their bodies took charge and started warring with their spirits. The apostle Paul clearly describes this problem when he exclaims, "For I do not do what I want, but I do the very thing I hate" (Rom. 7:15b). In his book *Miracles*, C. S. Lewis describes this condition as "estrangement" and envisions a day "when nature and Spirit are fully harmonised—when Spirit rides nature so perfectly that the two together make rather a *Centaur* than a mounted knight" (p. 161).

The primary means that the Holy Spirit uses to heal this estrangement is our practice of the spiritual disciplines. When we fast, we are telling our body that matters of the spirit are important. Serving another person puts his or her needs ahead of ours. In simplicity we are freed from the tyranny of always getting our own way. Worship reminds us that we are "dust." The spiritual disciplines put our bodies in a place where God can work his goodness into us and bring harmony into our lives.

And when our bodies and our spirits start to come back into harmony, we do away with categories. We easily move between religious and everyday activities, treating them as of equal value because God is present in both. And all that we say, all that we do, all that we are becomes a means to make God's presence real to those around us.

When our life is a "seamless garment," we are free to reveal God to the world. Wholly available to God, we become his representative, his emissary, and he does his work through us. Our mind becomes the mind of God helping his children understand his love. Our hands become the hands of Jesus nursing the sick. Our voice becomes the voice of Christ proclaiming the good news of the kingdom of God. Our arms become the arms of the Holy Spirit loving the sinner unconditionally. As we let the power and life of God flow through us, we become the person he created us to be and God becomes known to the world through us.

How does it make you feel to think that God works through you to do his work in the world? Describe your thoughts and feelings.

Reflection Question
Give each member a chance to respond to this question if he or she wishes.

Again, choose a member to read these paragraphs.

PRACTICING THE INCARNATIONAL TRADITION

Up to this point in the session we have been talking in abstract terms. That is the easiest approach to a subject such as incarnational living, which centers on the interior more than on the exterior—centers on who people are more than on what they do or say. Now, though, we need to move to the concrete, to practical changes that help us integrate our divided self. In that process of integration, the Incarnational Tradition forces us to change the interior first; it looks to the source of what we do and say.

We first start cooperating with the Holy Spirit rather than resisting. Most of us put up a barrier that excludes God, even though we are his children. We might think of this as an invisible shield, an extra layer of protective skin that we cover ourselves with to keep God out. When we pray, "God, I remove this barrier; I ask you to penetrate my life and make me whole," God responds and energizes us.

We start thinking about life as a harmonious unit, abandoning such distinctions as spirit/matter, sacred/secular, faith/work, soul/body, religious/worldly as we move toward integration. Jesus showed us by his actions that life can be unified and seamless, that we can move readily in the power of God every day of the week, not just on "holy" days.

We consider our vocation to be as much a "calling" as that of minister or priest or religious. In the carpenter's shop Jesus served God when he served other people, making tables and chairs and cradles. We similarly serve God by helping a woman select a dress or answering a man's question about telephone service or filling an order for a book.

We view the family as a place where God can be served rather than as a means to fulfill our own needs and wants. All of us desperately need to make connection with other people, to feel needed and loved. The family meets those needs and more. This view of family life may catapult us into service that some think is demeaning, but we find God even while we change diapers and wash windows.

We stop thinking in terms of what comes first or who is on top or what is most important. A truly integrated person brings God, family, and vocation together, spending time with each as needed rather than as dictated by a legalistic scheme such as ten minutes with God, two hours with the family, and eight hours at work. Since the CEO and the secretary are equally valuable, equally precious, equally loved by God, we respect and treat each person equally. All of our actions and activities are important in God's economy, because we show forth the presence of God to the world.

We remember that our interior transformation takes time and occurs gradually. In concert with the other Traditions—Contemplative, Holiness, Charismatic, Social Justice, and Evangelical—the Incarnational Tradition leads us deeper into the interior and guides our actions so that we can truly bring the presence of God to those in our family, in our work, and in our society. Through us the invisible world of the spirit becomes visible.

EXERCISES IN THE INCARNATIONAL TRADITION

Have each member read over the exercises silently, or have members read them aloud, one at a time. Spend a few moments considering them as each person chooses the exercise he or she will do before the next meeting.

1. *Take an inventory of your life.*
   List on a piece of paper all of the activities that you are involved in, such as work, church, clubs, housework, parenting, hobbies, sports. Be very specific; if you belong to two clubs, for example, list both. Now, on a scale of 1 to 10 (with 1 representing the least effective), decide how well you bring the presence of God into each activity. Do not be discouraged if the results are disappointing. Even for people who have been practicing the disciplines for quite a while, change takes time. Pray, asking God to help you show forth his presence in those areas that have lower scores. Then, as you participate in the activities, imagine God working through you.

2. *Remove the barrier that keeps God outside.*
   As you sit in a chair, imagine that you have an extra layer of skin (or even full-body armor) that keeps God's Spirit out of the innermost parts of your being. Hold this image in your mind for a moment. Then destroy or rip off the barrier and invite the Spirit of God to penetrate you, to overwhelm you with his love, to take up permanent residence in your body, to make you a "tabernacle." Continue sitting quietly until you feel that the work is complete, expressing your gratitude when it is done.

3. *Do your work in honor of God.*
   In our culture we do things to honor famous people—roasts, awards, ceremonies, parades. Choose a day this week to do your work in honor

of God. When you go to work, drive your car in a manner that brings respect to God. As you answer the telephone, give the conversation and its results to God. While planting a tree, thank God for the beauty of his creation. Conduct your staff meeting as if God were *visibly* present—an audience of One—observing everything that you do.

4. *Read a book by Dostoyevsky, Tolstoy, or Solzhenitsyn.*
Fyodor Dostoyevsky, Leo Tolstoy, and Aleksandr Solzhenitsyn masterfully wove their Christian faith into their literary works. Dostoyevsky writes about a Christ-figure, Prince Mishkin, in *The Idiot*. Tolstoy's *War and Peace* and *Anna Karenina* engage us in the great struggles of human souls from war to peace and love. The contemporary writer Solzhenitsyn integrates his faith into the warp and woof of *One Day in the Life of Ivan Denisovich* and *Cancer Ward*. If you feel a little overwhelmed by Dostoyevsky's and Tolstoy's writings, take more than one week to read one of their books, or read *One Day*.

5. *Receive the sacrament of Communion or Eucharist.*
On Sunday attend a church that will be serving Communion. Prepare to receive the sacrament by taking a mental inventory of ways God has helped you bring his presence into your family, workplace, and social contacts during the past six days. Then receive the Eucharist joyfully, knowing that Jesus Christ is truly present to you and longs to strengthen you and teach you daily. Say a prayer of thanksgiving for his presence in your life and ask him to be with you during the coming week.

ENDING AND BEGINNING

Our Father, who art in heaven,
Hallowed be thy name.
Thy kingdom come,
Thy will be done,
On earth as it is in heaven.
Give us this day our daily bread;
And forgive us our trespasses
As we forgive those who trespass against us.
And lead us not into temptation,
But deliver us from evil.
For thine is the kingdom, and the power, and the glory, forever and ever.
Amen.

Allow each member time to share which of the above exercises he or she plans to do during the week. Encourage each other in this venture. After everyone has shared, join hands in a circle and pray the Lord's Prayer aloud and in unison.

Ask for a volunteer to lead the next meeting. Tell people to bring at least one photocopy (per person) of the Worksheet found on pages 103–104 to the next meeting.

Discovering a Practical Strategy for Spiritual Growth

THE SPIRITUAL FORMATION GROUP

THE FOOTPRINTS OF GOD

At our last meeting each of us agreed to try one of the exercises in the Incarnational Tradition. Let's share our experiences by answering the following question:

What did you learn about God and about yourself while doing the exercise?

JESUS AND OUR LIFE TOGETHER
Gospel Passage: Matthew 18:19–20

"Again, truly I tell you, if two of you agree on earth about anything you ask, it will be done for you by my Father in heaven. For where two or three are gathered in my name, I am there among them."

Reflection Question

How do you think Jesus' followers felt when they heard these words?

THINKING IT THROUGH

Jesus tells his followers that he will be in their midst each time they gather in his name. Far from leaving them on their own, Jesus promises his disciples that he will be with them forever. Christ is with us as well, when we gather "in his name." Because Jesus Christ called us to become disciples, he is always at the center of our corporate gatherings. He is the reason we come together.

If Jesus had simply died and left his followers to fend for themselves, Christian gatherings—whether large worship services or small-group fellowships—would be focused on the individuals who make up the groups. But quite the opposite is true: Christ rose from the dead, so our fellowships focus on him. It is Christ who calls us, Christ who empowers us, and Christ who unites us.

It is very easy to focus on our needs, our failures, our efforts to "get right" with God, but our worship must center on Christ. Jesus reminds us that our power and authority come from him. When we come together and agree on something, Christ assures us that God will do it.

The word "agree," however, means more than simply coming to a decision. The Greek word used here, *symphoneo*, implies a harmony that is achieved only through prayer and searching. Like a symphony, we are to practice and to work together, and to pray until we are in tune. The unified voice we lift in prayer comes before the Father through the Son, who has promised to answer our pleas.

When we gather in Jesus' name, we are not merely remembering Jesus because of what he said and did; we are actively encountering the living Christ because of what he has done and continues to do among us.

Why is it so easy to focus on ourselves rather than on what Christ is doing among us?   **Reflection Question**

GOD AND THE SPIRITUAL FORMATION GROUP

How do people grow in the spiritual life? One major way is to do spiritual exercises—that is, to practice the spiritual disciplines—within the framework of a Christian fellowship. These exercises help us grow spiritually by creating space in our lives where God can begin to transform us. Many times we erect "No Trespassing" signs to block God's entrance into the areas of our lives that most need remolding and reshaping. Other times we think we are simply too busy to include God in our lives.

Have one member of the group read this entire section.

God has chosen spiritual exercises as the primary way to build our relationship with him. From the Bible we discover that the activities we have been learning about and doing—prayer, fasting, service, and so on—serve as instruction manuals that God uses to teach us how to live holy lives.

Spiritual growth occurs when we focus on God and practice the disciplines. God loves us and wants to teach us, heal us, bless us, encourage us. He has chosen these and countless other exercises as a way to remove our "No Trespassing" signs, to enter our lives and reshape them.

Earlier we noted that these exercises are best practiced in fellowship with other Christians. There are three reasons for this. First, for our own sakes God does not want us to isolate ourselves from each other as saints and to grow further and further apart; rather, he desires that we embrace each other as sinners and grow closer and closer together. The possibilities of sin will remain with us, no matter how far we travel in the Christian life, but traveling with kindred spirits will make those possibilities less appealing. Traveling together on the path of transformation will also help us avoid the pitfall of turning the disciplines into deadly, self-righteous practices. We are fellow travelers, fellow sinners united in Christ's body.

Second, God understands that we have more strength to do what is best for us when involved in a loving fellowship. Isolated and alone, we yield easily to apathy; together and united, we can resist all the forces that attack us, including indifference. In Hebrews we read, "And let us consider how we may spur one another on toward love and good deeds" (10:24, NIV). We benefit from spurring one another on. That is why God gave us the wonderful gift of Christian community.

Third, God knows that we need guidance. From time to time we all need help in discerning what to do. Are we doing too much? Too little? Are we on the right path? Do we need to be patient? Sometimes we cannot hear an answer because we are too close to the situation. Since God often uses other people to give guidance to his children, quite often we find our answer in listening to others as they share their experiences of failure and success. The Christian fellowship provides guidance as we look to one another for help.

Reflection Question
Allow each person a few moments to respond to this question.

Of the three needs listed below, which is your most urgent?

- *To grow closer to others*
- *To be encouraged by others*
- *To learn from others*

WHAT IS A SPIRITUAL FORMATION GROUP?

As before, have a member read this entire section.

A few years ago a Princeton University poll revealed that the number-one priority for most Christians was "personal spiritual growth." In spite of this need, most churches do not have intentional plans to meet their members' desires for spiritual growth. Recognizing our own need, we have been taking small steps toward consistent spiritual growth in the previous seven sessions, and we are preparing to take larger steps in the future. We have also been assembling the many pieces of the Spiritual Formation Group mosaic—pieces that we are now ready to put in place.

The Spiritual Formation Group is a Christian fellowship whose purpose is to encourage its members to practice the spiritual disciplines. It is not a prayer group, though it incorporates prayer. It is not a support group, though support is found there. And it is not a Bible study, though the Bible is used by the group. It is a group that focuses on what God has done, is doing, and will do in our lives as we begin practicing the spiritual disciplines.

Overall, a Spiritual Formation Group answers the question, *What will help me grow spiritually?* while each meeting of a Spiritual Formation Group focuses on two issues: *What has God been doing in my life?* and *What do I plan to do before the next meeting to make space for him to do even more?* So what is the process involved in these groups?

First, we bring the strengths from the Six Traditions we have studied—Contemplative, Holiness, Charismatic, Social Justice, Evangelical, and Incarnational—into an intentional community: the Spiritual Formation Group. This balanced approach, coupled with Christian fellowship, helps us maintain equilibrium in our spiritual lives.

Second, we are provided with material to help start the Spiritual Formation Group. This book provides the structure for starting a Spiritual Formation Group and a plan to continue meeting beyond the initial nine sessions. The concluding chapter of *A Spiritual Formation Workbook* contains ideas and exercises to give the direction we all need and answers a question that stymies many of us: "What am I supposed to do?"

Third, the Spiritual Formation Group provides mutual encouragement and accountability. By joining forces, by "synergizing" energies, the group becomes greater than the sum of its individual members. Each person receives power and energy from the group (as well as from the Lord) to practice the spiritual disciplines.

This is what happens in a Spiritual Formation Group.

Which of these three pieces do you need the most?

- *Balance and community*
- *Structure, ideas, and exercises*
- *Encouragement and accountability*

Reflection Question
Give each member a chance to respond to this question if he or she wishes.

WORKING TOGETHER AS A SPIRITUAL FORMATION GROUP

For the past seven weeks we have worked together as a Spiritual Formation Group. At each meeting we have individually chosen an exercise, made a covenant with the group members to do an exercise before the next gathering, and shared our experiences with each other during our next time together. This is how a Spiritual Formation Group works together. Now we are ready to take the next step.

The Order of Meeting gives each gathering of a Spiritual Formation Group a step-by-step structure. It is not intended to control or inhibit a group; rather, it is an outline to help a leader open, guide, and close the regular meeting.

For each meeting a group must choose a leader. (There is no single leader in a Spiritual Formation Group; everyone shares the leadership.) Guiding the group through the Order of Meeting is the leader's only responsibility. It is a good idea to decide who will lead the next meeting at the close of each gathering.

Ask everyone to turn to page 99 (the section titled "Order of Meeting") and to keep a finger in this section as they will be turning back to it later. Members will read aloud from the Order of Meeting as prompted by the leader, who begins by reading these paragraphs.

Opening Words

The leader reads this paragraph, then asks a member to read the section on page 99 titled "Opening Words."

The leader chosen by the group at the end of the previous gathering begins each meeting by reading the Opening Words. These words gather the group together, give it focus, and remind each member of the importance of preserving confidentiality. Some groups choose to read the words exactly as printed; others find a paraphrase helpful. Either way, the Opening Words are important, because they set the right tone at the beginning of each meeting.

Covenant

The leader reads this paragraph, then asks the members to read the section on page 99 titled "Covenant" aloud and in unison.

Next, the group turns its attention to the Covenant. This too reminds us of the group's purpose. Founded on Jesus Christ as Savior, Teacher, Lord, and Friend, it helps us grow spiritually. In addition, reading the Covenant aloud affirms our intention to "seek continual renewal through spiritual exercises, spiritual gifts, and acts of service"—an intention based, of course, on our faith in Jesus Christ.

Common Disciplines

The leader reads this paragraph, then chooses one person to read the section on page 100 titled "Common Disciplines," or asks group members to take turns reading one each.

During the third section of the meeting we read the Common Disciplines. These brief statements based on the Six Traditions give substance to our pledge to seek continual spiritual renewal.

Questions of Examen

The leader reads this paragraph, then chooses one person to read the section on page 100 titled "Questions of Examen," or asks group members to take turns reading one each.

Over the past few weeks we have become familiar with the fourth section, "Questions of Examen" (or Reflection Questions) under the heading "The Footprints of God." These questions are designed to help us share what God is doing in our lives. No one is expected to answer all six sets of questions or all of the questions within a set; everyone responds to those that apply to the exercises he or she did since the group's last meeting. However, people who see God working in their lives in another area may choose to answer one or more of the other questions.

Looking Ahead

The leader reads these paragraphs.

The next section is titled "Looking Ahead." After we have discussed our past exercises, we make plans for the week ahead. All members are asked to select one or more areas to work on, to choose an exercise that will help them move forward, and then to share their intention with the rest of the group.

We may want to give extra support to each other by recording each person's intent.

This planning time is crucial. We need to offer guidance, support, and accountability to each other; and these things can be done only when we make clear and definite plans and share them with each other. Remember: If we fail to plan, we plan to fail.

In order to plan effectively, we need to become familiar with the "Ideas and Exercises" and "Worksheet" sections of this workbook.

Ideas and Exercises

The section titled "Ideas and Exercises" lists the Six Traditions that we practice in order to expand those areas in our spiritual lives. Under each Tradition are ideas and exercises that we can do as we continue meeting with our Spiritual Formation Group. This section provides the hints and helping hand that most of us need now and then.

The leader reads this paragraph.

Worksheet

On photocopies of the lined Worksheet, you and each member of the group can record what everyone is doing. At each meeting fill in the date at the top; then, as members share their intentions, record their plans beside their names. You may then fill in your own plans as well. This simple exercise is a powerful motivational tool; we become aware of what exercises others are doing, and they become aware of what exercises we are doing. In the process, we experience guidance, encouragement, and accountability.

After asking everyone to look over the section titled "Ideas and Exercises" (starting on page 86) and the section titled "Worksheet" (starting on page 103), the leader reads this paragraph.

Ending and Beginning

The sixth section of each meeting—the section that we have been calling "Ending and Beginning"—is titled "The Lord's Prayer" in the Order of Meeting. It focuses on supportive prayer for each member of the group. We are asked to share needs and situations that would benefit from prayer. It is helpful to write the concerns that are mentioned at the bottom of the Worksheet so that we can remember to pray for them during the course of the coming week. Most groups then choose one or more members to lead the group in praying for those concerns during a short time of intercessory prayer. When this prayer is finished, we pray aloud and in unison the Lord's Prayer.

After asking everyone to turn back to the Order of Meeting and to look over the section titled "The Lord's Prayer" (page 101), the leader reads this paragraph.

Closing Words

Finally, the leader closes the meeting by reading the Closing Words. Just as the meeting began with a reminder of the importance of maintaining confidentiality, so it ends with the same reminder.

The leader reads this paragraph, then asks a member to read the section on page 102 titled "Closing Words."

READY TO FLY SOLO

The leader asks the members to turn back to this section (page 80) and reads these paragraphs.

Congratulations! We have gone through the Order of Meeting and know how a Spiritual Formation Group works. Now choose one exercise from Sessions 2 through 7 that you have not done in the "Exercises in " sections and determine to do it between now and the next meeting. On the photocopy of the Worksheet that you brought today, write down what you and the other members of the group are planning to do.

When we meet the next time, we will use the Order of Meeting as our guide. We have completed the Eight Beginning Sessions and are ready to have a regular meeting. At the end of our next meeting we will turn to the section titled "Periodic Evaluation" and use it to evaluate our group (what we liked, what we did not like, what we would like to change, and so on) or schedule a separate time when we can do it together. When we have completed the Periodic Evaluation, we will decide if we want to continue meeting as a group and if we want to continue using this method. If we agree to continue gathering regularly, we will covenant to meet and to work together as a group for the next six months.

May the ever-living Jesus Christ who is in our midst bless us and keep us until we meet again.

ENDING AND BEGINNING

Allow each member time to share which of the exercises he or she plans to do during the week. Encourage each other in this venture. After everyone has shared, join hands in a circle and pray the Lord's Prayer aloud and in unison.

Our Father, who art in heaven,
Hallowed be thy name.
Thy kingdom come,
Thy will be done,
On earth as it is in heaven.
Give us this day our daily bread;
And forgive us our trespasses
As we forgive those who trespass against us.
And lead us not into temptation,
But deliver us from evil.
For thine is the kingdom, and the power, and the glory, forever and ever.
Amen.

If the Periodic Evaluation will be done at the end of the next regular meeting, ask for a volunteer to lead the gathering who is willing to take notes. Also, ask all members to read the Periodic Evaluation in the coming week and to prayerfully consider their response to each question. If the Periodic Evaluation will be done at a separate gathering, ask for two volunteers: one to lead the regular meeting and one to lead the special evaluation session.

Periodic Evaluation

EVALUATING THE GROUP'S EXPERIENCE AND PLANNING FOR THE FUTURE

WHY EVALUATE?

In order for a small group to function effectively and continue to meet the needs of its members, it is crucial that the group periodically evaluate itself.

WHAT EVALUATION DOES

Group evaluation accomplishes several things:

- *It restores vitality.*
  Small groups have a tendency to slip into routines that make their meetings seem mundane. By evaluating the group's dynamics, it is possible to restore the original vision and rekindle the initial enthusiasm.

- *It overcomes problems.*
  It is easy for a small group to develop relational or directional problems that slowly begin to undermine its effectiveness. By evaluating the way the group is working together to meet its goals, it is possible to repair some of these areas and to establish a more efficient structure.

- *It gives people a chance to share their needs and concerns.*
  A group's most common ailment is the unvoiced concern. When a group is no longer meeting our needs, we have a tendency to keep that fact to ourselves and simply stop attending. Later, when the other members learn that we have decided to quit, they are shocked and

If this evaluation is being done in a separate meeting, turn to the section titled "Order of Meeting" (page 99), follow the outline through the Opening Words and Covenant, and return to this point. The leader then reads this section. If the evaluation is being done at the end of a regular meeting, begin at the Spiritual Formation Group Evaluation Questionnaire on page 82 after following the Order of Meeting outline through the "Looking Ahead" section.

surprised. Evaluation helps us share our current needs and offers us a graceful way to quit without hurting anyone's feelings.

WHEN TO EVALUATE

Ask one member of the group to read this entire section.

The following evaluation form should be used after a Spiritual Formation Group has met for an introductory gathering meeting, gone through the Eight Beginning Sessions in this workbook, and held one regular meeting. Some groups center a special meeting around the evaluation; others conduct the evaluation at the conclusion of the first regular meeting. It is far less important *when* groups evaluate themselves, however, than *that* they do so.

The Spiritual Formation Group is designed for a six-month "covenant period." This mutually agreed-upon time span is long enough for the members to become acquainted with how a Spiritual Formation Group works yet short enough to keep it focused. A six-month covenant to work together, with the agreement that group members will do an evaluation at its end, also allows members to fully experience mutual fellowship and encouragement before making a decision to meet for another six months.

Existing groups who have never done an evaluation should do one as soon as possible. This will help the members define the group and determine where it is going. While we recommend that new and existing groups do an evaluation every six months, it is certainly possible for them to evaluate themselves at any time.

The following questionnaire contains questions that will help each member share his or her feelings about the group. It is important that everyone have a chance to speak; answering the questions one at a time will encourage members to respond. The person who volunteered to lead the meeting at which evaluation takes place guides the evaluation process.

SPIRITUAL FORMATION GROUP
EVALUATION QUESTIONNAIRE
Personal Questions

Allow each person a few moments to answer each question if he or she wishes.

1. Given that one of my goals is to become a better disciple of Jesus Christ, has this Spiritual Formation Group . . .

    A. *Increased my effectiveness substantially?*

    B. *Increased my effectiveness in small ways?*

    C. *Made no difference in my effectiveness?*

2. Do the same "wheel" exercise that we did in Session 1.

    Below, the Six Traditions are arranged around the spokes of a wheel. Using a scale of 1 to 10 (with 1 being the least proficient and closest to the center of the wheel), estimate where you are in each area on the wheel spokes. Place dots at those points; then connect the dots from spoke to spoke to form a ring around the center.

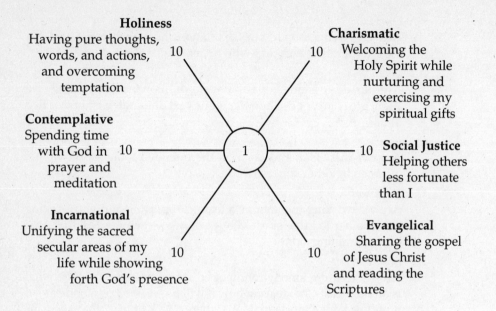

Compare this wheel to the one on page 30; then answer questions 3 and 4.

3. In which of the Six Traditions (or areas of discipleship) have I seen the most growth?

    A. *In the contemplative, or prayer-filled, life*

    B. *In the holiness, or virtuous, life*

    C. *In the charismatic, or Spirit-empowered, life*

    D. *In the social justice, or compassionate, life*

    E. *In the evangelical, or Word-centered, life*

    F. *In the incarnational, or sacramental, life*

4. In which of the Six Traditions (or areas of discipleship) have I seen the least growth?

    A. *In the contemplative, or prayer-filled, life*

    B. *In the holiness, or virtuous, life*

    C. *In the charismatic, or Spirit-empowered, life*

    D. *In the social justice, or compassionate, life*

    E. *In the evangelical, or Word-centered, life*

    F. *In the incarnational, or sacramental, life*

The leader guides the discussion, keeping in mind that some members may hesitate to share their feelings about the Spiritual Formation Group. He or she reminds members to be kind and honest, and takes notes of the suggestions and decisions made.

Group Questions

1. Discuss each of the following areas by answering the question under each heading.

   A. *Direction*
      Are we moving toward our destination and reaching our goals, or are we wandering around with no real sense of direction?

   B. *Balance*
      Are our discussions equally balanced, allowing each member a chance to share, or do they sometimes get dominated by one or two of us?

   C. *Focus*
      Are our discussions focused on the intended topic, or do we get diverted by other concerns?

   D. *Teamwork*
      Are we working together as a team, supporting and encouraging one another to grow spiritually, or do we sometimes feel that each of us is training alone?

   E. *Environment*
      Are we creating an environment where we feel free to share what is on our hearts, not fearing how it will be received or wondering if it will be kept confidential, or is there a lack of trust that keeps us from sharing from the heart?

   F. *Attendance*
      Are all of us attending our meetings as faithfully as we can, or are some of us failing to attend regularly?

   G. *Hospitality*
      Are we willing to welcome new people into the group, or would a new person feel uncomfortable or unwanted?

   H. *Time*
      Are we keeping within our time limit, or do our meetings last too long?

2. If you could keep only one thing about this group exactly the way it is, what would it be?

3. If you could change only one thing about this group, what would it be?

4. From what we have discussed,

   A. Should we continue as a group? (If yes, how many months should we commit to meet?)

   B. Should we change anything about the group? (If yes, what changes should we make?)

MAKING A COVENANT

- Who will lead the next meeting (name)?
- When will we meet (time, day, frequency)?
- Where will we meet (location)?
- How long will the meetings last (minutes)?
- What is our new covenant period (months)?
- When will we do the next evaluation (date)?

If your group has decided to continue meeting, you may want to use "Making a Covenant" to create a covenant that specifically defines the terms and length of your commitment. You may also wish to have all of the members sign the notes taken by the leader as another way to confirm your covenant.

Our group is now functioning as an ongoing, supportive Spiritual Formation Group. May God bless us as together we "grow in the grace and knowledge of our Lord and Savior Jesus Christ" (2 Peter 3:18a).

If the evaluation was done as part of a regular meeting or a separate meeting, the leader reads this paragraph before guiding the group back to the section titled "Order of Meeting" and closing with the Lord's Prayer (page 101).

Ideas and Exercises

We all struggle to live the Traditions day by day. Discovering new activities that are rooted in the spiritual disciplines and the Traditions is a key part of our spiritual growth. Every week we need to incorporate one exercise into our weekly plans. The following exercises, divided into the six areas of discipleship that we have been studying, are only representative of the many different activities that help us go forward in the spiritual life. Since these ideas are simply *suggestions* and contain no rules or standards, feel free to modify them to fit your needs and situation. Full publication information for all books mentioned in these exercises can be found in the Bibliography on page 105.

Before presenting these suggestions, though, we have five cautions.

CAUTION I: Avoid vague goals.

SOLUTION: Make your goals *measurable* (for example, "Read one chapter from the Bible each day").

CAUTION II: Don't try to do the impossible or unprofitable.

SOLUTION: Be sure that your plan is *attainable*. Ask your group, "Is this too much for me to try?"

CAUTION III: Don't distance yourself from the exercises.

SOLUTION: *Personalize* the activities by doing them frequently and trying new ones often.

CAUTION IV: Refrain from procrastination.

SOLUTION: Make *specific* plans now (for example, "Meet God in prayer every morning at 7:30").

CAUTION V: In spite of Cautions I and IV, avoid becoming rigid or legalistic.

SOLUTION: Be *flexible* when planning by focusing on the interior practice, not the exterior activity.

And above all, remember that "when we fail to plan, we plan to fail."

PRACTICING THE PRAYER-FILLED LIFE:
THE CONTEMPLATIVE TRADITION

1. Pray for ten minutes each morning or evening.

2. Pray without words (in silence) for five minutes each day.

3. Offer a short prayer throughout the day (for example, the hesychastic prayer "Lord Jesus Christ, have mercy on me, a sinner" or the verse "Create in me a clean heart, O God, and put a new and right spirit within me" [Ps. 51:10]).

4. Set aside an hour that will be free of distraction. Use the time for solitude, prayer, and meditation on the Bible.

5. Read a section from a devotional classic such as Augustine's *Confessions*, Brother Lawrence's *The Practice of the Presence of God*, or Madame Guyon's *Experiencing the Depths of Jesus Christ*. (See *Devotional Classics*, a volume in the RENOVARÉ Resources for Spiritual Renewal, for other suggestions.)

6. Write out a prayer in your journal. You may wish to keep it private, or you may wish to share it with your group. Write the letter as if it were addressed to God, telling him how you feel.

7. Learn to appreciate God through his creation. Take a walk in a park or simply sit and watch a sunset. Consider the majesty of the world, giving thanks and praise for all of God's creation.

8. Set aside fifteen minutes for a time of thanksgiving. Thank God for everything you can think of. Do not worry about intercession or confession; this is a time simply to give thanks.

9. Practice the art of listening to God. Meditate on a verse of Scripture, being attentive to what God wants to tell you. Note the words in the verse. Does anything stand out? Turn the verse into a prayer. Ask God to teach you during this time of silence.

10. Hold people and situations before God in prayer. Take ten minutes a day to bring your friends and loved ones before God. Do not worry about words; simply imagine Jesus standing beside them before the throne of grace. Let God minister to all of their cares and hurts.

11. Pray for the leaders in your church. Find a time this week to pray specifically for your pastors and other leaders. Ask God to give them strength and wisdom and compassion. Pray for their protection.

12. Try "flash prayers." When you see someone—anyone—silently pray for that person. Riding on a bus, standing in a line, sitting in a room— wherever you are, inwardly ask the Lord to give those around you joy, to touch their lives with his presence.

13. See if you can wake up praying. Give your day to God in that prayer, asking him to guide you through each meeting, each conversation, each appointment.

14. Take a "prayer walk" this week. Choose crowded urban streets where you can bless many passersby with prayer, or go to a park or woods where you can rediscover that the earth and everything in it is the Lord's.

15. Pray as you jog, swim, or play tennis. Bless the homes you pass as you run or head for the pool or court. Thank God for your swimming friends. Even try praying for your tennis opponent!

Other Ideas

1. _____

_____

2. _____

_____

3. _____

_____

4. _____

_____

5. _____

_____

6. _____

_____

7. _____

_____

8. _____

_____

9. _____

_____

PRACTICING THE VIRTUOUS LIFE:
THE HOLINESS TRADITION

1. Work on taming your tongue; speak only when necessary.

2. Try a twenty-four-hour fast to discipline your appetite. Eat no food from one lunch to another, skipping both dinner and breakfast. Modify the fast by drinking fruit juice and plenty of water. Use the time you save by not eating to read your Bible.

3. Resolve to overcome temptation with silence and prayer. Instead of fighting or running from temptation, stand in silence, praying for God to give you strength.

4. Fast from the television for a week. Many people find television programs addictive, and they are certainly time-consuming. By not watching television for a week, you will be able to discern its effect upon your life. Again, use the time you gain to try some other spiritual discipline or simply to enjoy your family, perhaps playing a game or taking a walk together.

5. Be a "gossip-buster." Whenever you or someone you are with begins to gossip, quickly end it. Guide the conversation to a different subject.

6. Practice the art of speaking positively. Resolve to make two positive remarks about someone or something for every negative remark you make. Be careful not to get too far in debt!

7. Spend ten minutes each morning thinking about good things. Discipline your thoughts until they readily focus on the true, the honorable, the just, the pure, the pleasing, the commendable (Phil. 4:8).

8. Memorize the Ten Commandments (Exod. 20:2–17). These laws were sweeter than honey to the Psalmist (Ps. 19:10). Memorize them as a way to make them a more conscious part of your daily life.

9. Write out a confession in your journal. One of the best ways to get back on track after wrongdoing is to confess the things you have done or left undone. Be honest. God knows your faults and failings—you will not be telling him anything he does not already know! The exercise is for your benefit, not God's.

10. Cultivate integrity in your speech by focusing on simplicity and honesty in all that you say. Watch for guile and deception, which can creep into your speech in subtle ways. Be ruthless as you seek to tell the truth in everything.

11. Do a "covet" check in your life. Are you enviously desiring anything? The Tenth Commandment tells us not to covet our neighbor's possessions. Unchecked, covetousness leads to constant turmoil. Make a "wish list" of all the things you would like to have, and then destroy the list while asking God to help you let go of your desire to possess. Finally, offer a prayer of thanksgiving for all that you have.

12. Do a "treasure" check in your life. Are there things that you prize too much? Jesus warned us not to place our hope in things that will decay and perish. The rich young ruler of Luke 18:18–30 kept all the commandments but lacked one thing: the ability to let go of his wealth. If you cannot freely give a treasure away, maybe it possesses you more than you possess it. Give it away and experience the freedom that comes when you relinquish a treasure.

13. Keep the Sabbath. "Remember the sabbath day, and keep it holy" is one of the most neglected of the Ten Commandments (Exod. 20:8). The Sabbath is actually God's gift to a frazzled world. Sit down with your family and discuss how you can set one day (usually Sunday) aside for rest and recreation. Refuse to do any work—even the catch-up housework that presses you. Resist the guilt and simply rest in God. Allow yourself permission to do nothing, absolutely nothing.

14. Set aside an hour for "holy leisure." Find an hour when you can nap on a couch, or lie in a hammock, or relax over a coffee. God, who made us and realizes that we need rest, will bless our "holy leisure."

15. Read *The Pursuit of Holiness*, a bestseller by Jerry Bridges that reveals the undiluted truth about sin, temptation, and the unparalleled freedoms that come from saying no.

Other Ideas

1. _____

_____

2. _____

_____

3. _____

_____

4. _____

_____

5. _____

_____

6. _____

_____

PRACTICING THE SPIRIT-EMPOWERED LIFE: THE CHARISMATIC TRADITION

1. Search the Scriptures to discover your spiritual gifts. Romans 12:6–8 and 1 Corinthians 12:8–11 list gifts that we are to strive for and exercise as members of the body of Christ. Read the passages, pray about them, and seek understanding. You may want to read a book on the subject. Donald Gee's *Concerning Spiritual Gifts* is a good introduction.

2. Explore the "Spirit-empowered" roles. Ephesians 4:11–13 lists several leadership positions in the Church. Read the passage, asking the Spirit to direct your thinking to how you can best serve the body of Christ.

3. Pray for the Holy Spirit. Jesus said that we must "ask" for the Holy Spirit (Luke 11:13). Do you feel that the Spirit is present and active in your life? If not, spend an hour this week in prayer, asking the Lord for the Holy Spirit's real and life-giving presence.

4. Spend time reading about the "fruit" of the Spirit. Galatians 5:22–23 lists the fruit, or "virtues," of the Spirit. The presence of that fruit is a sure sign that God's Spirit is working in your life. Choose one fruit that you would like to see increase in your life, pray for its increase, and seek ways you can nurture its growth.

5. Bless others with your "fruit." What fruit of the Spirit is most evident in your life (Gal. 5:22–23)? This week consciously be a conduit for the love, joy, peace, patience, kindness, generosity, faithfulness, gentleness, and self-control that the Spirit has given you.

6. Allow the Holy Spirit to become part of your prayer life. When you are praying this week, ask the Spirit to intercede when you cannot find words to express your concerns and your joys.

7. Welcome the illuminating work of the Spirit. One of the Spirit's functions is to make the words of the Bible come to life. When reading the Scriptures this week, open your mind to the "divine Interpreter."

8. Put on your armor. As Christians, we are given divine equipment called the "armor of God" (Eph. 6:10–17). List the different pieces of armor and ask the Spirit which one you need most at this time. When the answer comes, ask the Spirit to add this piece to your array of virtues so that you can withstand the devil's attacks.

9. Exercise your spiritual gifts. If you have discovered your spiritual gifts (see exercise 1), spend an hour this week exercising them in your local church.

10. Seek others' counsel about how you can best use your spiritual gifts. The Spirit sometimes gives guidance through other people. Ask a few friends whom you trust and who know you well what they see as your spiritual gifts and how they see those gifts best used. From this exercise you may reach a new awareness (or confirm an old one) concerning your service in the body of Christ.

11. Really *worship* when you go to church this week. Walk in the door with "a spirit of thanksgiving." Sit in silence prior to the service. Meditate on God's mercy and majesty. Sing the hymns with enthusiasm. Fill the sanctuary with prayer. Above all, praise God. You may find that this practice infects the people sitting around you with joy and thanksgiving.

12. Study the Scripture passages about the Holy Spirit. Use a concordance or a chain-reference Bible to find verses that refer to the Holy Spirit—his nature, role, and deeds. Highlight those references that you find new and exciting.

13. Pray for the Spirit to give you confidence in the promises of God in Christ. Begin by reading Romans 8. The Holy Spirit is able to verify your position as a child of God the Father. Let the Spirit teach you how to pray to God as his child, saying "Abba, Father," and give you a life of confidence before God.

14. Read Tony Campolo's book *How to Be Pentecostal Without Speaking in Tongues*. It is an excellent introduction to the charismatic life, focusing on the "vital aliveness" found in charismatic communities while avoiding the excesses found in every Tradition.

15. For fifteen minutes a day this week, wait on the Holy Spirit. Allow the Spirit to come into every corner of your life—your secrets, your desires, your failings, your victories, your all.

Other Ideas

1. _____

    _____

2. _____

    _____

3. _____

    _____

4. _____

    _____

5. _____

    _____

PRACTICING THE COMPASSIONATE LIFE: THE SOCIAL JUSTICE TRADITION

1. Write a supportive letter this week to someone you feel may be needing a word of encouragement.

2. If you live with others, help out around the house. This may seem minor, but household chores are usually done grudgingly. Your willingness to do more than your share of work will be a real service to the others in the household.

3. Spend an afternoon working at a local shelter or soup kitchen. Your help is sorely needed, even if you can only sweep floors.

4. Donate blood. We are giving the gift of life when we give blood. Call your local blood bank and set up an appointment.

5. Recycle your trash. Caring for the environment is an issue of social justice. Recycling what you throw away increases the next generation's chance for a bright future.

6. Help a friend in need. Do you know someone who needs assistance? If so, help that person, whether the task is hanging wallpaper, grocery shopping, helping with a move, or fixing the roof. Volunteering to help is a simple way to care for your neighbor.

7. Write to your member of Congress—senator or representative—and share your views. Is there an issue that you feel strongly about? Be sure that you have the facts straight and are expressing genuine Christian concern, not just prejudice.

8. Join a prison ministry. Your local church should know about groups that regularly minister to prisoners (and their families) in your area. Contact such a group and go with them to visit the inmates, who often feel forgotten in their isolation. Jesus told us that when we visit inmates, we are visiting him (Matt. 25:31–46).

9. Address an injustice with compassion. Is someone being treated unfairly? Do not be silent when your words could make a difference.

10. Practice the service of hiddenness. Do a kind deed (for example, shoveling snow from a sidewalk or calling on nursing home residents) without being asked or expecting recognition.

11. Serve others with your words. Protect people's reputation and speak well of others as a way of serving them. Kind words are great deeds.

12. Serve others by letting them have "space." We sometimes overwhelm people or consume their time or usurp their freedom with our expectations. Make a concerted effort to give people space. Ask them what they want to do or if they want to be alone or if they are free to talk before imposing your expectations upon them.

13. Serve others by letting others serve you. Are you guilty of not letting other people do things for you? Hold a door? Buy a cup of coffee? Make a photocopy? This is a sin. It is a gift to others to let them serve you; do not deny them this joy.

14. Read a book that discusses social justice issues. As an example, *The Politics of Jesus* by John Howard Yoder forces readers to ask hard questions. You may also want to read Donald Kraybill's book *The Upside-Down Kingdom*. Though you may not agree with everything these authors say, they should stimulate your thinking.

15. Write a one-page response this week to the following question: What is the most pressing social justice issue today, and what position should I, as a Christian, take? Share the paper with the other members of your Spiritual Formation Group.

Other Ideas

1. _____

   _____

2. _____

   _____

3. _____

   _____

4. _____

   _____

5. _____

   _____

6. _____

   _____

7. _____

   _____

PRACTICING THE WORD-CENTERED LIFE: THE EVANGELICAL TRADITION

1. Read the Bible for fifteen minutes a day. Choose a method of reading (for example, tackling a chapter or a section a day) and follow it. Let the Bible influence the course of each day.

2. Meditate on John 1:1. Write the verse on several three-by-five cards and put them on your bathroom mirror, on the dashboard of your car, and in places where you spend a lot of time. As often as possible, pause, read the verse, and meditate on the mystery of Jesus Christ as the living Word of God.

3. Ponder John the Baptist's role. Read John 1:6–9 several times, paying particular attention to what John was to Jesus (a "witness") and what his task was (to "testify" about Jesus). Consider how John's example can help you be more assertive in your proclamation of the gospel.

4. Read a chapter of the Bible before falling asleep. Reading from the Bible just before we retire for the night is a nice way to end the day. It also helps us awaken with the word of God on our minds. You may want to read the chapter aloud with your children or your spouse or your college roommate.

5. As you carry out your regular activities this week, think about the following question: How has my newfound understanding of Jesus as the living Word of God affected the practice of my faith? Record your response in your journal.

6. Talk about your faith in Jesus Christ with a relative or close friend. Often we neglect to talk about our faith with the most important people in our lives!

7. Meditate on a psalm once a day. The psalms are wonderful prayers that help us commune with God. Let the words of the psalms be your words. Read them slowly, over and over, until they become your prayers.

8. Meditate on the mystery of God entering history. Read John 1:14, remembering that "Word" in this verse refers to Jesus Christ. The apostle John writes that "the Word became flesh." Hold this mystery before God and ask him to help it take root in the deepest recesses of your soul.

9. Make a real effort to reach others with the message of Christ. When you are talking with someone, guide the conversation into issues that affect you deeply, such as life, death, meaning, and so on. Ask the person how he or she feels. If you discern little interest, politely drop the subject. But if you sense a yearning to hear more, freely share what Christ means to you.

10. Memorize a verse or passage of Scripture. Some people like to memorize "theme" verses (for example, verses that relate to God's power). Choose a verse (or even two or three) and recite it to your Spiritual Formation Group during the next meeting.

11. Describe the "living Word" in your own words. First read the description of Jesus' eternal and physical life that is recorded in 1 John 1:1–3 several times. Then put the same thoughts into your own words, writing them in your journal.

12. Get acquainted with one of your neighbors. Simple friendliness can often afford opportunities to share God's goodness.

13. Study the Bible. Use a Bible that has study notes or get a good commentary and delve deeply into a passage, a chapter, or an entire book.

14. Read Revelation 1:12–20. When John saw the living Christ, he fell at his feet as though dead. How do you respond to Christ's presence? With fear? dread? confusion? awe? gratitude? Thank God for sending Jesus Christ to be our ever-living Savior, Teacher, Lord, and Friend. If you experience fear or dread or confusion about Christ's role, ask God to replace those feelings with love.

15. Rediscover the gospel of Jesus Christ. Read Peter's sermon on the day of Pentecost in Acts 2:14–36 and answer these questions, writing them on a piece of paper: Who was Jesus? What did he do? What is the proof? What were the results? Now write down how your answers should affect your life.

Other Ideas

1. _____

   _____

2. _____

   _____

3. _____

   _____

4. _____

   _____

PRACTICING THE SACRAMENTAL LIFE: THE INCARNATIONAL TRADITION

1. Choose a day this week to do everything in honor of God. Drive your car, answer the telephone, conduct the staff meeting, greet people, and enter data in the computer to an audience of One.

2. Receive the sacrament of Communion or Eucharist. Attend a church that will be serving Communion. Receive Eucharist joyfully, knowing that Jesus Christ is truly present to you and longs to strengthen and teach you daily.

3. Read *One Day in the Life of Ivan Denisovich*. Aleksandr Solzhenitsyn integrates his faith into the warp and woof of *One Day*, following in the tradition of novelists Fyodor Dostoyevsky and Leo Tolstoy.

4. Remove the barrier that keeps God outside. Imagine that you are wearing full-body armor that keeps God's spirit out of the innermost parts of your being. Remove it, invite God in, and wait until you feel that the work is complete, giving thanks at the end.

5. Help your church organize an art show. Artists—painters, potters, photographers, sculptors, weavers, and others—creatively express the *imago Dei*, the image of God, through their art. Some of the greatest artists ever were Christian. Organize an art show of the work done by members of your fellowship.

6. Read *The Journal and Major Essays of John Woolman*. Woolman was an eighteenth-century tailor, businessman, and minister of Christ whose tender conscience and persuasive manner awakened the hard hearts of colonial Americans to the evils of slavery. Woolman's life is a stellar example of how the Incarnational Tradition works.

7. Attend a service at a synagogue on the Sabbath. It is difficult to understand many of the stories in the Gospels unless we become familiar with the Jewish faith. Pay special attention to the liturgical aspects of the service.

8. Attend a Christian church outside your tradition. If you belong to a liturgical church (for example, Catholic, Anglican, Lutheran), attend a "free church" on Sunday—and vice versa. Participate fully, feeling and absorbing the presence of God in the songs, prayers, sermon or homily, and sacraments.

9. Bring the presence of God to the ill. Contact a nursing home and make arrangements to visit the patients. Most homes have a lounge where mobile, cognizant patients read and watch television; perhaps you can talk with them there. As you converse with a patient, place your hand on his or her arm or hand, open yourself to God, and ask God to fill the patient with his presence.

10. Listen to Handel's *Messiah*. This glorious oratorio has endured for over two hundred years and broken down the sacred/secular walls in the world of music. Listen to a recording of the complete work, paying particular attention to the words that flowed out of George Frideric Handel's faith.

11. Bring God into your workplace by asking him to help you solve problems. This communication does not need to be formal; quick, silent prayers spoken before or during a telephone conversation or meeting are heard by God too.

12. Bless your home. If you have not already done so, walk through your house and bless each room. Most of us spend the majority of our lives in our homes and fail to invite God into them.

13. Visit with children. If children live in your neighborhood, make a special effort to engage them in conversation. Young children are so transparent that they help us see God.

14. Take God with you wherever you go. During the next few days make a special effort to be a "tabernacle" where God dwells. Cooperate with God to bring good wherever you walk—in the park, in your home, in your church—by praying for those you meet.

15. Invite God to your mealtimes. For one week, make a special effort to sense the presence of the risen Lord during your mealtimes with other people. It is important to open a meal with prayer; prayer that takes place *during* a meal should be silent unless special concerns are voiced that would benefit from prayer.

Other Ideas

1. _____

   _____

2. _____

   _____

3. _____

   _____

4. _____

   _____

5. _____

   _____

Order of Meeting

I. OPENING WORDS

Welcome to the RENOVARÉ Spiritual Formation Group [or other chosen name]. May God's Holy Spirit bless us, and may we find fellowship and encouragement during this time together.

Remember, we gather together with one purpose—to become better disciples of Jesus Christ. We do this by encouraging one another to keep Jesus' word, which, as he said, is what we naturally do when we love him (John 14:23–24). Through the grace of mutual accountability, we strive to inspire one another to love and good works.

Please keep in mind that everything said here is to be held in confidence. Only then can we feel free to share openly and honestly. All hopes and dreams, all fears and failures—even our joys and successes—are to stay within these walls. This is how we help each other.

After a few moments of collective silence, the leader for the week reads the Opening Words aloud.

II. COVENANT

In utter dependence upon Jesus Christ as my ever-living Savior, Teacher, Lord, and Friend, I will seek continual renewal through

- Spiritual exercises
- Spiritual gifts
- Acts of service

As a group, read the Covenant aloud and in unison.

III. COMMON DISCIPLINES

Beginning with the leader, take turns reading the Common Disciplines aloud until all six disciplines have been read.

- By God's grace, I will set aside time regularly for prayer, meditation, and spiritual reading and will seek to practice the presence of God.
- By God's grace, I will strive mightily against sin and will do deeds of love and mercy.
- By God's grace, I will welcome the Holy Spirit, exercising the gifts and nurturing the fruit while living in the joy and power of the Spirit.
- By God's grace, I will endeavor to serve others everywhere I can and will work for justice in all human relationships and social structures.
- By God's grace, I will share my faith with others as God leads and will study the Scriptures regularly.
- By God's grace, I will joyfully seek to show forth the presence of God in all that I am, in all that I do, in all that I say.

IV. QUESTIONS OF EXAMEN

Beginning with the leader, each member shares his or her experiences from the previous week. The Questions of Examen (or Reflection Questions) can be used to help focus the discussion. As time permits, encourage each member to answer at least the first question beside each bullet.

- In what ways has God made his presence known to you since our last meeting? What experiences of prayer, meditation, and spiritual reading has God given you? What difficulties or frustrations have you encountered? What joys and delights?
- What temptations have you faced since our last meeting? How did you respond? Which spiritual disciplines has God used to lead you further into holiness of heart and life?
- Have you sensed any influence or work of the Holy Spirit since our last meeting? What spiritual gifts has the Spirit enabled you to exercise? What was the outcome? What fruit of the Spirit would you like to see increase in your life? Which disciplines might be useful in this effort?
- What opportunities has God given you to serve others since our last meeting? How did you respond? Have you encountered any injustice to or oppression of others? Have you been able to work for justice and *shalom?*
- Has God provided an opportunity for you to share your faith with someone since our last meeting? How did you respond? In what ways have you encountered Christ in your reading of the Scriptures? How has the Bible shaped the way you think and live?
- In what ways have you been able to manifest the presence of God through your daily work since our last meeting? How has God fed and strengthened you through the ministry of word and sacrament?

V. LOOKING AHEAD

On which area or areas would you like to work this week? What specific exercise or exercises would you like to try?

Beginning with the leader, allow time for each member to share his or her plans for the coming week. These questions may be used as guidelines. Use copies of the Worksheet found on pages 103–104 of this workbook to record what you and the other members have chosen to do. Writing these commitments down will help you remember what others are doing and give you a chance to pray for them.

VI. THE LORD'S PRAYER

Our Father, who art in heaven,
Hallowed be thy name.
Thy kingdom come,
Thy will be done,
On earth as it is in heaven.
Give us this day our daily bread;
And forgive us our trespasses
As we forgive those who trespass against us.
And lead us not into temptation,
But deliver us from evil.
For thine is the kingdom, and the power, and the glory forever and ever.
Amen.

After each person has had a chance to share, the leader asks if anyone in the group has a particular need or knows of situations that would benefit from prayer. Members record these concerns on their Worksheets so that they can pray for them over the coming days. In addition, the leader invites someone to lead the group in prayer for those concerns. When the prayer is finished, members join hands in a circle and pray the Lord's Prayer aloud and in unison.

VII. CLOSING WORDS

At the conclusion of the Lord's Prayer, the leader ends the meeting by reading the Closing Words aloud and then asking for a volunteer to lead the next meeting.

Please remember that what we have said and heard in this gathering was spoken in confidence and should remain here when we leave. May the love, peace, and power of God be with us during this week. Amen.

For future convenience, you may wish to remove these Order of Meeting pages and have them laminated.

 # Worksheet

"And let us consider how we may spur one another on toward love and good deeds." (Heb. 10:24, NIV)

MY MEASURABLE, ATTAINABLE, PERSONAL, SPECIFIC PLAN

I plan to do the exercise(s) listed below _____ times between now and our next meeting. (You do not have to choose an exercise from all of the areas.)

_____ *Contemplative*

_____

_____ *Holiness*

_____

_____ *Charismatic*

_____

_____ *Social Justice*

_____

_____ *Evangelical*

_____

_____ *Incarnational*

_____

Date _____ Signed _____

This page may be photocopied for personal use.

OTHER MEMBERS' PLANS

Name _____   _____

_____

_____

Name _____   _____

_____

_____

Name _____   _____

_____

_____

Name _____   _____

_____

_____

"Cast all your anxiety on [God], because he cares for you." (1 Pet. 5:7)

Prayer concerns: _____

_____

_____

Other notes: _____

_____

_____

_____

This page may be photocopied for personal use.

Bibliography

Below is a brief description of the RENOVARÉ Resources for Spiritual Renewal and a listing of other books divided into specific areas of interest and the Six Traditions.

All of the RENOVARÉ Resources can be purchased at local bookstores; ordered from RENOVARÉ by writing 8 Inverness Drive East, Suite 102, Englewood, CO 80112-5624, sending a fax to 303-792-0146, or calling 303-792-0152; or secured on the Internet at http://www.amazon.com. Letters and faxes should contain name, full address (no. P.O. box numbers, please), type of credit card, number, expiration date, and name as it appears on the credit card.

Some of the other resources are also available at local bookstores or through RENOVARÉ or amazon.com. Others are out of print and available only through church and public libraries.

OTHER RENOVARÉ RESOURCES

Foster, Richard J. *Streams of Living Water: Celebrating the Great Traditions of Christian Faith.* San Francisco: HarperSanFrancisco, 1998. A spiritual history of the Church that explores the Six Traditions of Christian life and faith, examines the contribution of each, and seeks a balanced path to spiritual renewal by taking and practicing the best from each Tradition.

Foster, Richard J., and James Bryan Smith, eds. *Devotional Classics: Selected Readings for Individuals and Groups.* San Francisco: HarperSanFrancisco, 1993. Fifty-two readings from classic Christian devotional writers, each accompanied by a meditation, a linked Bible passage, questions, and exercises.

Griffin, Emilie. *Wilderness Time: A Guide for Spiritual Retreat*. San Francisco: HarperSanFrancisco, 1997. A step-by-step guide to the process of creating retreats from devotional writer Emilie Griffin, along with inspiration from her own extensive experience, practical tips, and a discussion of the importance of going apart to pray.

Janzen, Janet. *Songs for Renewal: A Devotional Guide to the Riches of Our Best-Loved Songs and Hymns*. San Francisco: HarperSanFrancisco, 1995. A collection of devotions rooted in music—African-American, American folk, gospel, traditional, and contemporary hymns and songs—taken from a rich array of Christian traditions.

Rea, Jana. *A Spiritual Formation Journal*. San Francisco: HarperSanFrancisco, 1996. Designed to accompany *A Spiritual Formation Workbook*, this book offers space for written reflection and prayer, inspiring quotes, questions, exercises, and worksheets.

Smith, James Bryan. *Embracing the Love of God: The Path and Promise of Christian Life*. San Francisco: HarperSanFrancisco, 1995. A distillation of basic principles of Christian love and a new paradigm for relationship with God, self, and others based on acceptance and care.

OTHER RESOURCES

The Spiritual Life

Foster, Richard J. *Celebration of Discipline: The Path to Spiritual Growth*. Rev. ed. San Francisco: HarperSanFrancisco, 1998.

Nouwen, Henri. *The Life of the Beloved*. New York: Crossroad, 1992.

Thomas à Kempis. *The Imitation of Christ*. Translated by William C. Creasy. Macon, GA: Mercer University Press, 1989.

Willard, Dallas. *The Spirit of the Disciplines: Understanding How God Changes Lives*. San Francisco: HarperSanFrancisco, 1988.

The Contemplative Tradition

Bounds, E. M. *Power Through Prayer*. Grand Rapids, MI: Zondervan, 1962.

Houston, James. *The Transforming Friendship: A Guide to Prayer*. Batavia, IL: Lion, 1989.

Merton, Thomas. *Contemplative Prayer*. Garden City, NY: Doubleday/Image, 1971.

Peterson, Eugene H. *Answering God: The Psalms As Tools for Prayer*. San Francisco: HarperSanFrancisco, 1989.

The Holiness Tradition

Bridges, Jerry. *The Pursuit of Holiness*. Colorado Springs, CO: NavPress, 1978.

Fénelon, François. *Christian Perfection*. Minneapolis, MN: Dimension Books, 1975.

Meilaender, Gilbert C. *The Theory and Practice of Virtue*. Notre Dame, IN: University of Notre Dame Press, 1984.

Packer, J. I. *Rediscovering Holiness*. Ann Arbor, MI: Servant, 1992.

The Charismatic Tradition

Bennet, Dennis, and Rita Bennet. *The Holy Spirit and You: A Study-Guide to the Spirit-Filled Life*. Plainfield, NJ: Logos, 1971.

Bruner, Frederick Dale. *A Theology of the Holy Spirit: The Pentecostal Experience and the New Testament Witness*. Grand Rapids, MI: Eerdmans, 1970.

Campolo, Tony. *How to Be Pentecostal Without Speaking in Tongues*. Waco, TX: Word, 1991.

Gee, Donald. *Concerning Spiritual Gifts*. Springfield, MO: Radiant, 1980.

The Social Justice Tradition

Hull, Gretchen Gaebelein. *Equal to Serve: Women and Men in the Church and Home*. Old Tappan, NJ: Revell, 1987.

Kraybill, Donald B. *The Upside-Down Kingdom*. Scottdale, PA: Herald, 1978.

Wallis, Jim. *The Call to Conversion: Recovering the Gospel for These Times*. San Francisco: HarperSanFrancisco, 1981.

Yoder, John Howard. *The Politics of Jesus*. Grand Rapids, MI: Eerdmans, 1972.

The Evangelical Tradition

Green, Michael. *Evangelism in the Early Church*. London: Highland Books, 1970.

Lewis, C. S. *Mere Christianity*. New York: Macmillan, 1943.

Mulholland, M. Robert, Jr. *The Power of Scripture in Spiritual Formation*. Nashville, TN: Upper Room, 1985.

Stott, John R. W. *Basic Christianity*. 2nd ed. Downers Grove, IL: InterVarsity, 1971.

The Incarnational Tradition

Griffin, Emilie. *The Reflective Executive: A Spirituality of Business and Enterprise*. New York: Crossroad, 1993.

Hammarskjöld, Dag. *Markings*. Translated by Leif Sjöberg and W. H. Auden. New York: Ballantine/Epiphany, 1983.

Moulton, Phillips P., ed. *The Journal and Major Essays of John Woolman*. Richmond, IN: Friends United Press, 1989.

Schmemann, Alexander. *For the Life of the World: Sacraments and Orthodoxy*. New York: St. Vladimir's Seminary Press/Athens, 1973.

Spiritual Formation Through Small Groups

Mallison, John. *Growing Christians in Small Groups*. Sydney, Australia: Scripture Union, 1989.

Pleuddemann, Carol, and Jim Pleuddemann. *Pilgrims in Progress*. Wheaton, IL: Harold Shaw, 1990.

Prior, David. *Parish Renewal at the Grass Roots*. Grand Rapids, MI: Zondervan, 1983.

Watson, David Lowes. *Accountable Discipleship*. Nashville, TN: Zondervan, 1967.

Additional Works Cited or Recommended

Augustine. *Confessions*. Translated by E. M. Blaiklock. Nashville, TN: Nelson, 1993.

Chambers, Oswald. *My Utmost for His Highest*. Greenburg, PA: Barbour, 1998.

Dostoyevsky, Fydor. *The Idiot*. Translated by Constance Garnett. New York: Bantam, 1983.

Guyon, Madame. *Experiencing the Depths of Jesus Christ*. Sargent, GA: Seedsowers, 1975.

Lawrence, Brother. *The Practice of the Presence of God*. Translated by John J. Delaney. New York: Doubleday/Image, 1977.

Lewis, C. S. *Miracles*. New York: Macmillan, 1960.

Solzhenitsyn, Aleksandr. *Cancer Ward*. Translated by Nicholas Bethell and David Berg. New York: Bantam, 1969.

———. *One Day in the Life of Ivan Denisovich*. New York: Bantam, 1984.

Tolstoy, Leo. *Anna Karenina*. Translated by Joel Carmichael. New York: Bantam, 1984.

———. *War and Peace*. Translated by Rosemary Edwards. New York: Viking, 1982.

⬤RENOVARÉ

RENOVARÉ (Latin meaning "to renew") was founded by Richard J. Foster and is an effort working for the renewal of the Church of Jesus Christ in all her multifaceted expressions. Christian in commitment, international in scope, and ecumenical in breadth, we seek to combine the best from the great Christian traditions with a practical strategy that nurtures spiritual growth.

These traditions include

Contemplative: The Prayer-Filled Life focuses upon intimacy with God and depth of spirituality. This spiritual dimension addresses the longing for a deeper, more vital Christian experience.

Holiness: The Virtuous Life focuses upon personal moral transformation and the power to develop "holy habits." This spiritual dimension addresses the erosion of moral fiber in personal and social life.

Charismatic: The Spirit-Empowered Life focuses upon the charisms of the Spirit and worship. This spiritual dimension addresses the yearning for the immediacy of God's presence among his people.

Social Justice: The Compassionate Life focuses upon justice and *shalom* in all human relationships and social structures. This spiritual dimension addresses the gospel imperative for equity and compassion among all people.

Evangelical: The Word-Centered Life focuses upon the proclamation of the evangel, the good news of the gospel. This spiritual dimension addresses the need for people to see the good news lived and hear the good news proclaimed.

Incarnational: The Sacramental Life focuses upon making present and visible the realm of the invisible spirit. This spiritual dimension addresses the crying need to experience God as truly manifest and notoriously active in daily life.

The practical strategy consists of:

Spiritual Formation Groups: These groups gather around the RENOVARÉ Covenant, Common Disciplines, and Questions of Examen (or Reflection Questions) and provide mutual encouragement and accountability to their members.

For more information about RENOVARÉ write to

RENOVARÉ
8 Inverness Drive East, Suite 102
Englewood, CO 80112-5624 USA